THE ALEXANDER SHAKESPEARE

Macbeth

Edited by

R. B. KENNEDY

PREFATORY NOTE

This series of Shakespeare's plays uses the full Alexander text which is recommended by many Examining Boards. By keeping in mind the fact that the language has changed considerably in four hundred years, as have customs, jokes, and stage conventions, the editors have aimed at helping the modern reader – whether English is his mother tongue or not – to grasp the full significance of these plays. The Notes, intended primarily for examination candidates, are presented in a simple, direct style. The needs of those unfamiliar with British culture have been specially considered.

Since quiet study of the printed word is unlikely to bring fully to life plays that were written directly for the public theatre, attention has been drawn to dramatic effects which are important in performance. The editors see Shakespeare's plays as living works of art which can be enjoyed today on stage, film and television in many parts of the world.

First edition 1972
Second edition 1983
Reprinted 1984, 1986, 1987, 1989, 1990 (twice), 1992, 1995, 1996

© Wm. Collins Sons and Co. Ltd.
London and Glasgow

ISBN 0 00 325253 1

Made and printed in Great Britain by
Scotprint Ltd, Musselburgh

A80269

Contents

An Elizabethan playhouse. Note the apron stage protruding into the auditorium, the space below it, the inner room at the rear of the stage, the gallery above the inner stage, the canopy over the main stage, and the absence of a roof over the audience.

THE THEATRE IN SHAKESPEARE'S DAY

On the face of it, the conditions in the Elizabethan theatre were not such as to encourage great writers. The public playhouse itself was not very different from an ordinary inn-yard; it was open to the weather; among the spectators there were often louts, pickpockets and prostitutes; some of the actors played up to the rowdy elements in the audience by inserting their own jokes into the authors' lines, while others spoke their words loudly but unfeelingly; the presentation was often rough and noisy, with fireworks to represent storms and battles, and a table and a few chairs to represent a tavern; there were no actresses, so boys took the parts of women, even such subtle and mature ones as Cleopatra and Lady Macbeth; there was rarely any scenery at all in the modern sense. In fact, a quick inspection of the English theatre in the reign of Elizabeth I by a time-traveller from the twentieth century might well produce only one positive reaction: the costumes were often elaborate and beautiful.

Shakespeare himself makes frequent comments in his plays about the limitations of the playhouse and the actors of his time, often apologizing for them. At the beginning of *Henry V* the Prologue refers to the stage as 'this unworthy scaffold' and to the theatre building (the Globe, probably) as 'this wooden O', and emphasizes the urgent need for imagination in making up for all the deficiencies of presentation. In introducing Act IV the Chorus goes so far as to say:

> . . . we shall much disgrace
> With four or five most vile and ragged foils,
> Right ill-dispos'd in brawl ridiculous,
> The name of Agincourt.'   (lines 49–52)

In *A Midsummer Night's Dream* (Act V, Scene i) he seems to dismiss actors with the words:

> 'The best in this kind are but shadows.'

3

Yet Elizabeth's theatre, with all its faults, stimulated dramatists to a variety of achievement that has never been equalled and, in Shakespeare, produced one of the greatest writers in history. In spite of all his grumbles he seems to have been fascinated by the challenge that it presented him with. It is necessary to re-examine his theatre carefully in order to understand how he was able to achieve so much with the materials he chose to use. What sort of place was the Elizabethan playhouse in reality? What sort of people were these criticized actors? And what sort of audiences gave them their living?

The Development of the Theatre up to Shakespeare's Time

For centuries in England noblemen had employed groups of skilled people to entertain them when required. Under Tudor rule, as England became more secure and united, actors such as these were given more freedom, and they often performed in public, while still acknowledging their 'overlords' (in the 1570s, for example, when Shakespeare was still a schoolboy at Stratford, one famous company was called 'Lord Leicester's Men'). London was rapidly becoming larger and more important in the second half of the sixteenth century, and many of the companies of actors took the opportunities offered to establish themselves at inns on the main roads leading to the City (for example, the Boar's Head in Whitechapel and the Tabard in Southwark) or in the City itself. These groups of actors would come to an agreement with the inn-keeper which would give them the use of the yard for their performances after people had eaten and drunk well in the middle of the day. Before long, some inns were taken over completely by companies of players and thus became the first public theatres. In 1574 the officials of the City of London issued an order which shows clearly that these theatres were both popular and also offensive to some respectable people, because the order complains about 'the inordinate haunting of great multitudes of people, specially youth, to plays, interludes and shows; namely occasion of frays and quarrels, evil practices of incontinency in great inns . . .' There is evidence that, on public holidays, the theatres on the banks of the Thames were crowded with noisy apprentices and tradesmen, but it would be wrong to think that audiences were always undiscriminating and loud-mouthed. In spite of the disapproval of Puritans and the more staid members of society, by the 1590s, when Shakespeare's plays were beginning to be performed, audiences consisted of a good cross-section of English society, nobility as well as workers, intellectuals as well as simple people out for a laugh; also (and in this respect English theatres were unique in Europe), it was quite normal for respectable women to attend plays. So Shakespeare had to write plays which would appeal to people of widely different kinds. He had to provide 'something for everyone' but at the same time to take care to unify the material so that it would not seem to fall into separate pieces as they watched it. A speech like that of the drunken porter in *Macbeth* could provide the 'groundlings' with a belly-laugh, but also held a deeper significance for those who could appreciate it. The audience he wrote for was one of a number of apparent drawbacks which Shakespeare was able to turn to his and our advantage.

Shakespeare's Actors

Nor were all the actors of the time mere 'rogues, vagabonds and sturdy beggars' as some were described in a Statute of 1572. It is true that many of them had a hard life and earned very little money, but leading actors could become partners in the ownership of the theatres in which they acted: Shakespeare was a shareholder in the Globe and the Blackfriars theatres when he was an actor as well as a playwright. In any case, the attacks made on Elizabethan actors were usually directed at their morals and not at their acting ability; it is clear that many of them must have been good at their trade if they were able to interpret complex works like the great tragedies in such a way as to attract enthusiastic audiences. Undoubtedly some of the boys took the women's parts with skill and confidence, since a man called Coryate, visiting Venice in 1611, expressed surprise that women could act as well as they: 'I saw women act, a thing that I never saw before . . . and they performed it with as good a grace, action, gesture . . . as ever I saw any masculine actor.' The quality of most of the actors who first presented Shakespeare's plays is probably accurately summed up by Fynes Moryson, who wrote, '. . . as there be, in my opinion, more plays in London than in all the parts of the world I have seen, so do these players or comedians excel all other in the world.'

The Structure of the Public Theatre

Although the 'purpose-built' theatres were based on the inn-yards which had been used for play-acting, most of them were circular. The walls contained galleries on three storeys from which the wealthier patrons watched; they must have been something like the 'boxes' in a modern theatre, except that they held much larger numbers – as many as 1500. The 'groundlings' stood on the floor of the building, facing a raised stage which projected from the 'stage-wall', the main features of which were:

1. a small room opening on to the back of the main stage and on the same level as it (rear stage);
2. a gallery above this inner stage (upper stage);
3. a canopy projecting from above the gallery over the main stage, to protect the actors from the weather (the 700 or 800 members of the audience who occupied the yard, or 'pit' as we call it today, had the sky above them).

In addition to these features there were dressing-rooms behind the stage and a space underneath it from which entrances could be made through trap-doors. All the acting areas – main stage, rear stage, upper stage and under stage – could be entered by actors directly from their dressing-rooms, and all of them were used in productions of Shakespeare's plays. For example, the inner stage, an almost cave-like structure, would have been where Ferdinand and Miranda are 'discovered' playing chess in the last act of *The Tempest*, while the upper stage was certainly the balcony

6

from which Romeo climbs down in Act III of *Romeo and Juliet*.

It can be seen that such a building, simple but adaptable, was not really unsuited to the presentation of plays like Shakespeare's. On the contrary, its simplicity guaranteed the minimum of distraction, while its shape and construction must have produced a sense of involvement on the part of the audience that modern producers would envy.

Other Resources of the Elizabethan Theatre

Although there were few attempts at scenery in the public theatre (painted backcloths were occasionally used in court performances), Shakespeare and his fellow playwrights were able to make use of a fair variety of 'properties'; lists of such articles have survived: they include beds, tables, thrones, and also trees, walls, a gallows, a Trojan horse and a 'Mouth of Hell'; in a list of properties belonging to the manager, Philip Henslowe, the curious item 'two mossy banks' appears. Possibly one of them was used for the

> 'bank whereon the wild thyme blows,
> Where oxlips and the nodding violet grows'

in *A Midsummer Night's Dream* (Act II, Scene i). Once again, imagination must have been required of the audience.

Costumes were the one aspect of stage production in which trouble and expense were hardly ever spared to obtain a magnificent effect. Only occasionally did they attempt any historical accuracy (almost all Elizabethan productions were what we should call 'modern-dress' ones), but they were appropriate to the characters who wore them: kings were seen to be kings and beggars were similarly unmistakable. It is an odd fact that there was usually no attempt at illusion in the costuming: if a costume *looked* fine and rich it probably *was*. Indeed, some of the costumes were almost unbelievably expensive. Henslowe lent his company £19 to buy a cloak, and the Alleyn brothers, well-known actors, gave £20 for a 'black velvet cloak, with sleeves embroidered all with silver and gold, lined with black satin striped with gold'.

With the one exception of the costumes, the 'machinery' of the playhouse was economical and uncomplicated rather than crude and rough, as we can see from this second and more leisurely look at it. This meant that playwrights were stimulated to produce the imaginative effects that they wanted from the language that they used. In the case of a really great writer like Shakespeare, when he had learned his trade in the theatre as an actor, it seems that he received quite enough assistance of a mechanical and structural kind without having irksome restrictions and conventions imposed on him; it is interesting to try to guess what he would have done with the highly complex apparatus of a modern television studio. We can see when we look back to his time that he used his instrument, the Elizabethan theatre, to the full, but placed his ultimate reliance on the communication between his imagination and that of his audience through the medium of words. It is, above all, his rich and wonderful use of language that must have made play-going at that time a memorable experience for people of widely different kinds. Fortunately, the deep satisfaction of appreciating and enjoying Shakespeare's work can be ours also, if we are willing to overcome the language difficulty produced by the passing of time.

INTRODUCTION

Macbeth is a simple play. That is to say, the plot is straightforward, the characters clearly presented, the opposition of good and evil perfectly plain. There is not even much doubt, at any stage, about the ultimate fate of Macbeth and his wife. In fact, a heavy sense of inevitability hangs over all their actions. Nevertheless, where so much is obvious, there is still a great deal of mystery. Why does this sturdy soldier become a mean killer and, worse, a hirer of thugs to do his killing for him, particularly when he knows, and says, that his plans are sure to bring retribution upon him? Why does Lady Macbeth, an apparently loving wife, see it almost as a duty to drive herself and her husband into evil ways? And why do so many quite good men allow this vicious couple to gain total power and ruin the state of Scotland?

Some aspects of the Macbeth story have become horribly familiar in the course of the history of our own century. Several modern dictators have begun as brave soldiers and ended as crazy destroyers, so that the line between legitimate warfare and power-hungry violence has become very blurred indeed. Psychologists have shown us that, behind seemingly straightforward human motives, good or bad, there are often extremely complicated emotions and intentions. For these and other reasons this play, now nearly four hundred years old, based on the life of a man who lived six hundred years before Shakespeare himself, still exerts a great fascination on audiences and readers all over the world. In the summing-up at the end of this book an attempt will be made to analyse the reasons for this continued interest, and to go more deeply into the questions raised in this introduction. In the meantime, those new to the play may care to consider some of the intriguing ingredients of the play they are about to study, particularly those that are likely to be evident on first seeing or reading it.

The witches These three sinister creatures introduce the play, in a very brief first scene. They intend to *meet with Macbeth,* and they immediately convey an impression of

9

impending horror. There is no clue to the nature of this horror, but we are uneasily aware of limitless possibilities. These agents of evil are at hand, ready to be consulted, ready to influence for the worse, for much of the play.

The good king King Duncan of Scotland soon appears, and impresses us with his integrity and generosity, as well as with his determination to do all he can for his kingdom's welfare. He is, in the early stages, the representative of goodness, trust and benevolent order.

The 'decent' men We are introduced to a number of Scotsmen – the *bleeding Sergeant*, the king's sons, Malcolm and Donalbain, Lennox, Ross, Banquo and Angus – who serve their king and country as well as they can. Under good leadership they are faithful and useful. They react in various ways to the kingship of the ruthless Macbeth.

The strongholds Much of the action takes place in the Scottish castles of Inverness, Forres, Dunsinane and Fife. These grim, grey containers of human turmoil provide effective settings for the deeds done. We are frequently reminded of their walls, battlements and heavy gates. The principal murders take place in or near them. Such deeds are partly hidden by their walls, or by darkness, or by both,

The weather The play starts with thunder, lightning, *fog and filthy air*; there is a moment of serene summer (seen through Duncan's innocent eyes), followed by a brooding, overcast night, breaking into unprecedented tempest (the night of the first murder). The evening of the banquet is also calm, but with the prospect of rain. Banquo dies and, soon after, the Macduff family is destroyed. During the rest of the play there is no direct description of the weather. The disturbances seem to reflect not only Scotland's time of trial but also the upheaval in Macbeth's mind. For most of the last two acts he is settled in and almost resigned to his own evil.

Scotland and England Scotland, suffering under Macbeth's tyranny, and England, an idyllic country under the saintly King Edward the Confessor, are vividly contrasted. But the essence of the contrast is not in any Scottish inferiority; rather, it is Scotland's sheer misfortune to have such an inexplicably evil ruler as Macbeth, and England's simple duty to help to destroy him.

Apparitions Apart from the witches themselves, there are several possibly supernatural elements in the play: the *air-drawn dagger* which Macbeth saw before he killed Duncan (though this might well have been the product of his own feverish imagination), the ghost of Banquo, and the things the witches conjure up for Macbeth's inspection at the beginning of Act IV. As a member of a modern audience, how would you explain these visions? Are they an embarrassment, or do they add to the horrible reality of the story?

The words of the play Finally, as you go through the play, it should be stimulating to notice how Shakespeare uses words to gain his effects. Unfortunately there are many words and phrases which require explanation to twentieth century readers (which is why notes are provided), but a little thought and imagination can make a great deal clear. The verse rhythms, the images, the descriptive words, even the punning and other forms of word-play, all add to the main impression: this is a tale of human evil and human goodness much of which appeals directly to us today.

After this brief outline of the main features of *Macbeth* we shall look more closely and intently at its constituent parts and examine the contribution each makes to the whole effect. After this analysis of the ingredients of the play, the 'Summing Up' (page 205) will attempt to put things together again and leave you better equipped to explore the play for yourself.

The Language of the Play

It has already been said that many Shakespearean words and phrases require explanation to twentieth century readers and play-goers. It is not at all surprising that a play written nearly four hundred years ago should present problems of understanding. Living languages are always changing and developing. Another difficulty is that playwrights have always interested and amused audiences by making topical references. An Elizabethan audience would have instantly recognized a mention of the Spanish Armada, or something relating to the contemporary troubles in Ireland, which people in a twentieth century theatre might not even notice. Although it must be said that much of what is most important 'gets across' quite readily, we can all gain more from a Shakespeare play by deepening our understanding of the text. But, however conscientiously readers follow any textual notes, they will only be adding to their comprehension of words and phrases. There is a broader strategy at work in Shakespeare's use of language that notes can only hint at. For example, the linguistic style often varies to suit the mood of the moment or the personality of the speaker. *Macbeth* begins with a heavy, menacing rhythm, a kind of incantation by the witches:

> *Fair is foul, and foul is fair:*
> *Hover through the fog and filthy air*
> (Act 1, Scene i, lines 12–13)

which breaks off suddenly and is replaced by a passage full of long, involved sentences of description and explanation. The wounded Sergeant tries to convey in detail to his king the reality of a terrible battle, and the almost superhuman impression that Macbeth's quality of fighting has made upon him. The Sergeant's account falters, he breaks off, exhausted, and the scene ends with a mixture of long, rolling lines and short, exclamatory ones. The news *seems* good: *The victory fell on us* (Act 1, Scene iii, line 59) says Ross, but the news of Cawdor's treachery is dismaying and the rhythms hint at confusion, not resolution. Ambiguous notes have been struck which condition our responses to what follows. As the play goes on, more doubts arise, and motives become obscure: these abstractions are reflected in the language. Macbeth and Lady Macbeth, when talking to themselves or to each other, are generally clear and direct in style:

Lady Macbeth: *Yet do I fear thy nature;*

> *It is too full o' th' milk of human kindness*
> *To catch the nearest way*
> (Act 1, Scene v, lines 15–17)

and

Macbeth: *He's here in double trust:·*
> *First, as I am his kinsman and his subject ...*
> (Act 1, Scene vii, lines 12–13)

Both of them, however, adopt a flamboyant, almost unctuous manner when they want to conceal their true feelings and intentions.

> *All our service*
> *In every point twice done, and then done double,*
> *Were-poor and single business to contend*
> *Against those honours deep and broad wherewith*
> *Your Majesty loads our house;*
> (Act 1, Scene vi, lines 14–18)

says Lady Macbeth. to Duncan, with murder in her mind, when welcoming him to the castle at Inverness. Her husband outdoes her in fulsome language, just after he has killed Duncan:

> *Here lay Duncan,*
> *His silver skin lac'd with his golden blood;*
> *And his gash'd stabs look'd like a breach in nature*
> *For ruin's wasteful entrance*
> (Act II, Scene iii, lines 111–14)

He goes on in such extravagant terms that (some critics suggest) Lady Macbeth has to pretend to faint in order to shut him up. Duncan and Banquo are almost the only characters whose true feelings are regularly reflected in their words. Even among some of those who represent the forces of goodness and truth, language is sometimes used to hide feelings rather than to express them. In the mysterious Act IV, Scene iii, Malcolm, who is to prove the saviour of Scotland, pours out hundreds of words of self-description, most of which he contradicts a little later on (*I ... unspeak mine own detraction*).

By Act V, clarity and directness have returned. Lady Macbeth, in her madness, speaks the simple words of truth:

> *Yet who would have thought the old man to have had*
> *so much blood in him?*
> (Act V, Scene i, lines 35–7)

Macbeth himself, face to face with ultimate reality, no
longer has any need for words as disguises:

> ... that which should accompany old age,
> ·As honour, love, obedience, troops of friends,
> I must not look to have.

(Act V, Scene iii, lines 24–6)

So, although it is apparent that language in this play
frequently reflects the moods and characters of the speakers,
it often does so in subtle ways. In addition, deeper and wider
impressions are being evoked, so that the language of the
play throughout reflects its underlying ideas: the onset of
evil fostered in human souls, doubt and insecurity (represented in ambiguous words) and finally the triumph of truth
and justice. Some further suggestions are made in the
Theme Index (page 214) about the use of particular words
by which these wide-ranging impressions are conveyed.

Plot

The story of the play may be set down in the following
matter-of-fact way:

Act I   A note of doubt and confusion is struck by three
witches in the first scene. They refer to a battle that
is not yet concluded; they plan to meet Macbeth,
one of the Scottish generals, in a deserted place, at
the end of the day's fighting. This is followed by a
scene in which Duncan, King of Scotland, hears an
interim report on the battle between the rebels
(Macdonwald and the Thane of Cawdor) together
with an army of Norwegian invaders, and the loyal
Scottish forces led by Macbeth and Banquo. A
wounded Sergeant describes a ferocious fight in
which both Macbeth and Banquo are acquitting
themselves with tremendous skill and determination.
Ross, another Scottish lord, comes in to announce
victory. King Duncan orders the execution of
Cawdor and the honouring of Macbeth with the
traitor's title.

       The witches meet Macbeth as they had planned.
Banquo, who is with him, addresses the witches with

suspicion, seeing them as probably evil. Macbeth
says little, but seems prepared to listen to them.
They greet him as Thane of Glamis (his correct
title), Thane of Cawdor (a title which, by now, is
his, but he doesn't know it), and future king. Banquo
notices that Macbeth reacts to what the witches say
with apparent fear. He orders the witches to make
some announcement about his future, too; they
respond by telling his fortune in riddles. In particular, they say that he is to be the ancestor of kings,
though not a king himself. The witches disappear,
leaving the two men, bewildered, repeating the
prophecies. Ross arrives to announce Macbeth's
new title of Thane of Cawdor. Macbeth's thoughts
turn at once to the possibility of being king, while
Banquo shows again that he deeply distrusts the
witches. (*What, can the devil speak true?*) Before the
end of the scene Macbeth is already contemplating
the murder of Duncan, though hoping that the final
prophecy may come true without any action on his
part.

In Scene iv, at the royal palace at Forres, King
Duncan and Macbeth face each other. The former is
warm, friendly, grateful for his general's services; the
latter superficially responsive and dutiful. Duncan
proclaims his son Malcolm as his heir. This leaves
Macbeth almost committed to the murder of
Duncan, but well aware of the nature of what he
contemplates (he refers to his *black and deep desires*).
In Scene v, Lady Macbeth makes her first appearance. She is reading a letter she has just received
from Macbeth in which he tells her about the
witches' prophecies, and the speedy fulfilment of
part of them. Lady Macbeth immediately determines
that he shall be king, by whatever means may be
necessary. She thinks he may be too good-natured
to *catch the nearest way* (that is, to kill Duncan),
but she feels confident that she can persuade him to
do it. Fate seems to be on her side when a messenger
enters to say that Duncan is on his way to honour
them with a visit. In a speech in which she reveals

much of her character (*The raven himself is hoarse...*,
lines 38–54), she acknowledges her natural womanly
feelings but appeals to the powers of darkness to
make her cruelly resolute. Macbeth arrives and his
wife makes it clear that she expects him to kill
Duncan that night. He makes no clear response.
Duncan and his court come to Inverness Castle and
are greeted effusively by Lady Macbeth but, significantly, not by Macbeth himself.

In the final scene of the first Act, Macbeth
struggles with his ambition and his conscience. He
has left the banquet hall where the king is dining to
try to work things out on his own. He knows that
Duncan is a good king, and is clear that nothing but
selfish ambition is pressing him towards a terrible
crime. He has just concluded that the plan is a
wicked one and that he will abandon it, when his
wife appears and attacks him viciously and deter-
minedly at his weakest point—his pride in his
own courage and manliness. She accuses him of
cowardice, and of not loving her. She follows this
up with an appalling demonstration that she is
willing to go to any lengths herself, declaring that
she would dash her own baby to the ground rather
than go back on her word. She outlines a plan of
action. Macbeth is persuaded, though he is dread-
fully aware of the wickedness of what they plan
to do.

Act II   Banquo, as well as Macbeth, seems to be plagued
by disturbing thoughts and temptations, but when
Macbeth suggests that they should meet to discuss
the witches' prophecies Banquo stresses that he will
do nothing dishonourable. Left alone, in another
agonized soliloquy (*Is this a dagger which I see
before me . . .?*) Macbeth shows how deeply dis-
tubed he is by the crime he is now committed to.
He hears the bell, struck by Lady Macbeth, which
is the signal for him to act; she has done her part
by giving Duncan's servants drink, to make them

sleepy. She hears Macbeth shout, and thinks that he has failed to kill the king, but he comes in saying that he has 'done the deed'. He seems shattered, and she has to stop him thinking about the crime and his lost honour. As before, she uses the weapon of scorn against him, but this time it does not work. He cannot bring himself to return to the king's room with the bloody daggers which he should have left there. She goes instead and smears the servants with blood. A thunderous knocking is heard. Macbeth is obsessed with the horror of Duncan's blood on his hands; Lady Macbeth, on the contrary, whose hands are now also red, dismisses it as unimportant (*A little water clears us of this deed*).

The porter of the castle is roused at last from his drunken sleep by the knocking. He staggers to the door of the castle to let in Macduff and Lennox, who have come to wake the king. Macbeth comes to see them, pretending that he has only just been awakened himself, and escorts Macduff to the king's apartment. After Lennox has commented on the wild weather, Macduff re-enters, so appalled that he can hardly say what he has seen. All the thanes and and the two princes, Malcolm and Donalbain, are roused. Lennox, Ross and Macbeth go back to the king's room, where Macbeth kills the two servants who are covered in blood. Soon afterwards Lennox blames these servants for the murder, but Macduff seems to have some doubts, since he asks Macbeth why he killed them. Macbeth begins to explain in an elaborate, overwrought manner and Lady Macbeth either faints or pretends to do so. Malcolm and Donalbain, who have hardly had time to feel anything except fear, decide to go away. Malcolm's words suggest that he already suspects Macbeth.

The final scene in the Act presents a picture of total disorder in the natural world, reflecting the chaos in human society. An old man describes bizarre events. Macduff says that Malcolm and Donalbain, because they have fled, are suspected of paying the servants to kill Duncan, their father.

He also says that Macbeth has been named as the new king; he is shortly to be crowned at Scone.

Act III Banquo clearly suspects that Macbeth has become king by foul means. Macbeth invites Banquo to a feast, and goes on to extract information from him about his planned movements in the afternoon. Because he is deeply concerned about the witches' prophecy that Banquo is to be the ancestor of kings, Macbeth is plotting to kill his comrade. As soon as he has said farewell to Banquo (*God be with you!*) he meets two murderers whom, with a strange mixture of lies, temptations, insults and compliments, he persuades to intercept Banquo as he returns towards the castle and kill him. Lady Macbeth tries to comfort her husband, who is full of gloom and fear but is not taking her into his confidence. He hints that he is arranging the removal of Banquo, the most obvious obstacle to his peace of mind. The murderers succeed in killing Banquo but, significantly, Fleance his son escapes.

While the banquet proceeds, the murderers tell Macbeth what has happened; he sinks again into gloom. Banquo's ghost enters and sits in Macbeth's seat. Macbeth, shaken with guilt and horror, creates a sensation among the guests and Lady Macbeth has to pretend that he often has such fits, which soon pass. The ghost disappears temporarily and Macbeth seems to recover, but when he proposes a toast to Banquo the ghost returns and Macbeth behaves like a madman. Lady Macbeth, worried that her husband will soon reveal his terrible secrets, ushers out the guests. Macbeth resolves to visit the witches and find out what his future holds. At the same time he contemplates even more frightful crimes (*Strange things I have in head that will to hand*).

After a brief and not very important scene in which Hecate, the witches' goddess, appears, two of the Scottish lords make it quite clear to each other that they strongly suspect Macbeth of the two murders. They reveal that Macduff has gone to the court of Edward the Confessor of England (where Malcolm, Duncan's son, is living) to beg his military assistance in opposing Macbeth.

Act IV Macbeth visits the witches who conjure up, first, a helmeted head; next, a bloody child; and then a crowned child with a tree in his hand. The first apparition warns him to beware of Macduff; the second says that no man born of woman can harm him; and the third informs him that he will never be defeated until Birnam Wood moves towards his castle at Dusinane. Macbeth is encouraged by the second and third prophecies but insists on putting a question to the supernatural powers about Banquo's descendants: will they ever rule Scotland? In answer he is shown a line of eight kings, accompanied by Banquo, whom they all resemble; the last king holds a mirror in which still more Banquo-like kings are visible. Immediately after this, news comes that Macduff has fled to England. Macbeth plans to attack his castle and slaughter his wife and entire family. In the next scene Lady Macduff has just been told by Ross that her husband has gone to England. She is angry and contemptuous of her husband and tells her small son that his father is dead. After a messenger has warned them that they are in danger, murderers sent by Macbeth enter and stab the son. We learn later that the whole family has been killed.

The scene switches to the English court where Malcolm and Macduff have a long and strange conversation. Macduff is urging Malcolm to return to Scotland to attempt to destroy Macbeth, but Malcolm is suspicious: he thinks Macduff (on Macbeth's behalf) may be trying to lure him back to Scotland. He tests Macduff by describing himself as a thoroughly wicked man, totally unsuited to be king in Macbeth's place. He wants to see if Macduff will go on encouraging him beyond all reasonable limits, in which case he will know that he is being

19

deceived. Up to a point Macduff accepts Malcolm's supposed vices, but eventually he despairs, says Malcolm is not even fit to live, let alone govern Scotland, and prepares to leave. This convinces Malcolm that Macduff is honest. When a doctor suddenly appears to tell them that King Edward is about to cure sick people by the laying on of hands, a new note of hope is introduced (the implication is that he will help Malcolm cure the social and political sickness in Scotland). Malcolm and Macduff are reconciled. Ross comes from Scotland with the appalling news of the destruction of Macduff's family and, after cursing himself for neglecting them, Macduff determines to seek revenge. The English army under Siward is ready and Malcolm, Macduff and Ross prepare to march northward.

Act V   The last Act begins with talk between a doctor and a gentlewoman about the serious illness of Lady Macbeth. We are told that she is in the habit of sleepwalking in a state of great agitation. She says things that seem to incriminate herself and her husband. Then Lady Macbeth herself enters with a lighted taper and the doctor prepares to record what she says. She appears to be washing her hands, and, in a fragmentary way, gives details of the murder of Duncan. She also refers to the killing of Lady Macduff and of Banquo. The watchers express their horror at the significance of what she has said.

A Scottish army is about to combine with the English forces under Malcolm and Siward, and attack Macbeth at Dunsinane. In Scene iii, Macbeth declares his desperate trust in the statements of the witches' apparitions: Birnam Wood cannot possibly move, and all men are born of women. Soon after this he is brought news of the approach of an army of ten thousand men; he sinks temporarily into a state of despair, seeing his own life as near its end.

The doctor tells him that there is no change in Lady Macbeth's state. Macbeth rouses himself and prepares for battle.

The combined army halts near Birnam Wood and Malcolm gives orders for the soldiers to camouflage themselves with leafy boughs cut from the trees. In Dusinane Castle Lady Macbeth's death is announced and Macbeth reacts by commenting on the meaninglessness of life. A messenger tells him that Birnam Wood is moving towards them. Macbeth flies into an almost insane rage, then lapses into weary resignation, and finally determines to die fighting. Two brief scenes follow (vii and viii) in which the battle is presented. Macbeth is still half-depending on the statement that he cannot be killed by any man 'of woman born' and, when he kills young Siward, is re-encouraged. He encounters the angry Macduff, who tells him that he was born by Caesarian section (i.e. cut from his mother's body). The last of the supernatural assurances is shown to be a deception. Macbeth refuses to fight Macduff and then, after all, decides to rely on his own strength and courage. They go off fighting. Soon afterwards Macduff returns with Macbeth's severed head. Malcolm ends the play by heralding a new era for his kingdom of Scotland.

Characterization

Even in such a prosaic summary of the plot, attitudes and relationships in the war between good and evil have to be presented and to some extent explained. In the process, certain characters stand out. It has often been said that Shakespeare's supreme achievement is in the depth and range of the characters he creates—that he constantly presents us with totally credible *individuals*. In most of his plays, certainly, the characters 'ring true'. Some of them are profound and convincing portraits, 'psychologically accurate', to use a familiar modern phrase. Shakespeare seems to have succeeded in creating *people*. He is assisted, of course, by the fact that we usually meet these characters as they are embodied by skilful actors and actresses. We watch a human being in the part, speaking the lines, frowning, moving, gesticulating. Gradually the illusion takes a grip upon us, our imaginations take over (guided by the imagination of the playwright) and we react for a time as though we are watching and listening to real people living their own real lives. In *Macbeth* there are certainly two characters who are presented skilfully, imaginatively and fully enough to have this effect upon us from the stage and, indeed, even from the pages of a book: Macbeth and Lady Macbeth. A good deal has. been said about them in this introduction already, but it may be helpful to say a little more. It has been pointed out that the play is one battle in the universal war of good and evil, and that the battle is not between thoroughly bad people and thoroughly good ones. Notwithstanding, by the middle of the play, Macbeth and his wife epitomize the evil which is feared and hated by almost everyone else and, by the end, it is virtually Macbeth versus the rest. The battle also goes on within the two chief characters. There is some danger of seeing them as figures in a sensational horror. story, but close attention dispels this tendency. We have to believe Lady Macbeth when she says that her husband is *full o' th' milk of human kindness* when we listen to what he says. No-one expresses the positive side of human nature more truly, from Macbeth's early comments on Duncan

> *this Duncan*
> *Hath borne his faculties so meek, hath been*
> *So clear in his great office, that his virtues*
> *Will plead like angels ...*

(Act I, Scene vii, lines 16–19)

to his poignant regrets at the end of his life

> *My way of life*
> *is fall'n into the sear, the yellow leaf...*

(Act V, Scene iii, lines 22–3)

How does a man who knows what human goodness is, and respects it, decline so rapidly into a murderous tyrant? Essentially, he chooses to do so, and *knows* that it is his choice, because of his ambition, the influence of a beloved wife, and the value he attaches to being thought a brave man. None of these aspects of his character is, in itself, evil,

22

but he allows himself to be led by them into evil. Ambition becomes an insatiable hunger, his love for his wife leads him to agree to frightful deeds, and his fighting quality degenerates into bloodlust. Accordingly, he alienates all our respect, yet evokes genuine pity at the last. We recognize a human being.

Lady Macbeth seems to alienate respect in playgoers and readers even more completely, and may not evoke pity, even at the end of her life. Yet she is, potentially, a 'partner in greatness' who, like Macbeth, takes it for granted that greatness is all that matters. Like so many other words in the play, this word is interpreted in various ways by various people. Lady Macbeth is a woman who will 'do anything' for her husband, just as he will 'do anything' for her. She is even willing, and able, to deny her own deepest feelings as a woman and a human being: it is at the moment when she declares that she would kill her own child rather than go back on her word that she inspires most repugnance; and it is at this moment that they are at one. It is the moment of commitment for both of them, and the signal for the train of events which plunges the whole of their society into tragic suffering. She is broken by it, and before long becomes a pathetic, deranged creature, as much a prey to guilt as Macbeth is.

No other character in the play is nearly as fully drawn as Macbeth and Lady Macbeth. Duncan is a good old man, reluctant to see evil in anyone. Malcolm is a tougher version of his father, and his personality seems at one point to veer towards interesting complexity (in the long conversation with Macduff at the English court). Banquo acts as a foil to Macbeth, as a man similarly tempted but too staunchly honourable to fall into evil ways himself—though he appears to do nothing to follow up his suspicions of Macbeth. Even Macduff, although he becomes the tyrant's executioner, does not develop into a particularly subtle personality, perhaps because we are not allowed to see him agonizing over the decision to leave his family and go to England. All these supporting characters revolve around Macbeth and Lady Macbeth, however. After Macbeth has died, we just feel confident that those who have survived will lead Scotland wisely and well.

Dramatic Structure and the Thematic Pattern

The first comment in this introduction was '*Macbeth* is a simple play'. This is particularly true of its dramatic structure and thematic pattern, both of which depend on the central issue of a struggle between good and evil. The play begins with a clear-cut physical conflict with, seemingly, no ambiguities. Scotland is a 'good' society ruled by a good man: the enemies are traitors, vicious invaders and contemptible mercenaries. Macbeth emerges as the champion of goodness and is immediately transformed into the enemy of goodness. Evil power proliferates, good men are destroyed, other good men run away. By Act IV, Scene iii, evil seems triumphant. Then Malcolm and Macduff reach agreement and the good King Edward lends his holy power. Faith and hope return and fortune swings away from evil. Act V shows the final battle. Scotland is cleansed and the new king acknowledges the need for supernatural goodness (*the grace of Grace*) to support human striving.

LIST OF CHARACTERS

DUNCAN, *King of Scotland*

MALCOLM
DONALBAIN } *his sons*

MACBETH
BANQUO } *Generals of the King's army*

MACDUFF
LENNOX
ROSS
MENTEITH } *Noblemen of Scotland*
ANGUS
CAITHNESS

FLEANCE, *son to Banquo*

SIWARD, *Earl of Northumberland, General of the English forces*

YOUNG SIWARD, *his son*

SEYTON, *an officer attending on Macbeth*

BOY, *son to Macduff*

A SERGEANT

A PORTER

AN OLD MAN

AN ENGLISH DOCTOR

A SCOTS DOCTOR

LADY MACBETH

LADY MACDUFF

GENTLEWOMAN *attending on Lady Macbeth*

THE WEIRD SISTERS

HECATE

THE GHOST *of Banquo*

APPARITIONS

LORDS, GENTLEMEN, OFFICERS, SOLDIERS, MURDERERS, ATTENDANTS, *and* MESSENGERS

THE SCENE: *Scotland and England*

NOTES

ACT ONE

SCENE I

The brief opening scene gives an immediate impression of mystery, horror and uncertainty. These witches would have been truly frightening to an audience, many of whom would have seen women burnt at the stake for selling themselves to the Devil. Macbeth is introduced by name by the Third Witch. What can these disgusting hags want with him?

3. *hurlyburly:* the confused noise of storm and battle. Thunder was produced for the Elizabethan stage by rolling cannon-balls. Nowadays the same effect is produced by shaking sheets of metal.
4. *lost and won:* the first of many apparent contradictions and confusions (see line 12 of this scene). The words can mean 'concluded one way or the other'.

9. *Graymalkin:* a name for a grey cat, which was a common familiar of witches. A familiar was a demon which attended and assisted a witch; these spirits usually took some rather sinister form.
10. *Paddock:* a toad. This is the Second Witch's familiar. Sounds were probably made off-stage to represent the calls of these familiar spirits, though it is difficult to imagine what sound a toad was supposed to make.
11. *Anon!* I am coming at once.
12. This line is a kind of motto for the witches. They delight in a reversal of all the normal values. Macbeth seems to involve himself with them by echoing the phrase, Act I, Scene iii, line 39.
13. *fog and filthy air:* this may have been produced by burning resin under the stage.

26

ACT ONE

Thunder and lightning.   Enter three WITCHES

First Witch
 When shall we three meet again?
 In thunder, lightning, or in rain?
Second Witch
 When the hurlyburly's done,
 When the battle's lost and won.
Third Witch
 That will be ere the set of sun.   5
First Witch
 Where the place?
Second Witch
 Upon the heath.
Third Witch
 There to meet with Macbeth.
First Witch
 I come, Graymalkin.
Second Witch
 Paddock calls.   10
Third Witch
 Anon!
All
 Fair is foul, and foul is fair:
 Hover through the fog and filthy air.

WITCHES vanish

27

MACBETH

SCENE II

For part of the second scene the feeling of uncertainty is maintained, because the outcome of the battle is left in doubt. The Sergeant, reporting his part of the battle, presents Macbeth as the decisive factor, and Ross gives the same impression from his point of view. We get a remarkable picture of Macbeth as a kind of superman, a fearless, ferocious, almost invulnerable champion of right against treachery.

1–3. *He can report . . . state:* He looks as though he has come, wounded, straight from the battle, and will be able to give us an up-to-date report.
5. *'Gainst my captivity:* to save me from being captured.
6. *knowledge of the broil:* news of the battle.
9. *choke their art:* (the two exhausted swimmers) prevent each other from using their swimming skill.
10. *to that:* to that end, i.e. to show that he is indubitably a traitor.
12. *swarm upon him:* like lice.
Western Isles: islands to the west, including Ireland and the Hebrides.
13. *kerns and gallowglasses:* lightly-armed foot-soldiers and horsemen armed with axes.
14–15. *Fortune:* the Roman goddess Fortuna, regarded as highly unreliable. Here she smiles on the cause she has already damned, behaving as treacherously as a prostitute (*whore*) might. Characteristically, Macbeth ignores her (*Disdaining Fortune*, line 17) and takes his fate into his own hands.
16. *that name:* the title *brave*.
17–18. *brandish'd steel . . . execution:* His sword steamed with the hot blood of those he had just killed.
19. *valour's minion:* the favourite of Valour (personified in much the same way as Fortune).
carv'd out his passage: cut his way through the men on the battlefield.
21. Macbeth had no time for civilities. He is a fighter who takes a brutally realistic view of war.
22–3. *Till he unseam'd . . . battlements:* he thrust his sword in at the navel (*nave*), ripped him open up to the jaws (*chaps*), then cut his head off and stuck it on the battlements.
24. *cousin:* Macbeth and Duncan were both grandsons of King Malcolm, but in any case the word *cousin* was often used by sovereigns of their noblemen.
worthy gentleman! What Macbeth has just done seems hardly gentlemanly, but there is no irony in Duncan's remark. Such actions in defence of king and country would have been regarded as truly worthy of one of gentle blood.
25–8. *As whence . . . Discomfort swells:* 'Just as storms fatal to ships burst out of the east, where the sun first shines, so danger springs from the place where everything seems well.' Although of course the Sergeant doesn't realize it, to the king these words could be a warning about Macbeth. Duncan regards him in this scene very much as a source of comfort, yet it will not be long before much *discomfort swells* from the same source.

SCENE II—*A camp near Forres*

> *Alarum within.   Enter* KING DUNCAN, MALCOLM, DONALBAIN, LENNOX *with* ATTENDANTS, *meeting a bleeding* SERGEANT

Duncan
What bloody man is that? He can report,
As seemeth by his plight, of the revolt
The newest state.
Malcolm   This is the sergeant
Who like a good and hardy soldier fought
'Gainst my captivity. Hail, brave friend!   5
Say to the King the knowledge of the broil
As thou didst leave it.
Sergeant   Doubtful it stood,
As two spent swimmers that do cling together
And choke their art. The merciless Macdonwald—
Worthy to be a rebel, for to that   10
The multiplying villainies of nature
Do swarm upon him—from the Western Isles
Of kerns and gallowglasses is supplied;
And Fortune, on his damned quarrel smiling,
Show'd like a rebel's whore. But all's too weak;   15
For brave Macbeth—well he deserves that name—
Disdaining Fortune, with his brandish'd steel
Which smok'd with bloody execution,
Like valour's minion, carv'd out his passage
Till he fac'd the slave;   20
Which ne'er shook hands, nor bade farewell to him,
Till he unseam'd him from the nave to th' chaps,
And fix'd his head upon our battlements.
Duncan
O valiant cousin! worthy gentleman!
Sergeant
As whence the sun gins his reflection   25
Shipwrecking storms and direful thunders break,

30. *Compell'd . . . heels:* Forced these unreliable soldiers to rely on running away.
31. *Norweyan:* an old form of Norwegian.
surveying vantage: seeing his chance. No doubt Duncan's troops had relaxed on seeing the kerns run away.
32. *With furbish'd arms:* 'having repaired their weapons' (or perhaps taken up new ones).

34-5. *Yes . . . the lion:* The Sergeant is being very sarcastic. 'Yes, they were about as dismayed as an eagle is by a sparrow, or a lion by a hare,' he says.
36. *sooth:* truth.
37. *as cannons . . . cracks:* Like cannons with double charges of gunpowder.

39-40. *Except they meant . . . Golgotha:* Unless they intended to bathe in the steaming wounds (of their enemies) or make the battle as grimly memorable a scene as the crucifixion of Christ.

43-4. *So well . . . both:* Your words and your wounds do you equal honour.
smack: taste.

45. *Thane:* a Scottish nobleman and landowner, often the chief of a clan.

47. *So should he . . . strange:* His appearance suggests that he has strange news to tell.

50-1. *Where . . . cold:* Where the Norwegian banners mock the (Scottish) sky and, as they wave, freeze our men with fear.
52. *Norway himself:* King Sweno of Norway.

So from that spring whence comfort seem'd to come
Discomfort swells. Mark, King of Scotland, mark:
No sooner justice had, with valour arm'd,
Compell'd these skipping kerns to trust their heels,   *30*
But the Norweyan lord, surveying vantage,
With furbish'd arms and new supplies of men,
Began a fresh assault.

Duncan   Dismay'd not this
Our captains, Macbeth and Banquo?

Sergeant   Yes;
As sparrows eagles, or the hare the lion.   *35*
If I say sooth, I must report they were
As cannons overcharg'd with double cracks;
So they doubly redoubled strokes upon the foe.
Except they meant to bathe in reeking wounds,
Or memorize another Golgotha,   *40*
I cannot tell—
But I am faint; my gashes cry for help.

Duncan
So well thy words become thee as thy wounds;
They smack of honour both.—Go get him surgeons.

Exit SERGEANT, *attended.   Enter* ROSS

Who comes here?

Malcolm   The worthy Thane of Ross.   *45*

Lennox
What a haste looks through his eyes!
So should he look that seems to speak things strange.

Ross
God save the King!

Duncan
Whence cam'st thou, worthy thane?

Ross   From Fife, great King
Where the Norweyan banners flout the sky   *50*
And fan our people cold.
Norway himself, with terrible numbers,
Assisted by that most disloyal traitor

54. *a dismal conflict:* one which filled the Scottish forces with foreboding.

55. *Bellona's bridegroom:* the bridegroom of Bellona, the Roman goddess of war. Macbeth is being compared with Mars, the god of war himself.

lapp'd in proof: clad in tried and tested armour.

56. *Confronted . . . self-comparisons:* Gave him something (i.e. a model of a fighting man) to compare himself with.

58. *Curbing his lavish spirit:* overcoming his insolent courage.

61. *craves composition:* begs for peace terms.

62. *Nor would we . . . men:* We would not allow him to bury his dead soldiers.

63. *disbursed:* paid.

Saint Colme's Inch: a small island in the Firth of Forth, now called Inchcolm. (St. Colme is another form of St. Columba.)

64. *dollars:* These coins were not minted until the early sixteenth century, 500 years after the time of Duncan and Macbeth. Does it matter that Shakespeare does not seem to have worried about such inaccuracy? Could it have had a deliberate purpose?

65–6. *deceive . . . interest:* treacherously attack our dearest interests.

pronounce his present death: order his immediate execution.

SCENE III

The meeting of Macbeth and the witches, which they foretold in Act I, Scene i, is about to take place. Before the victorious general, quite unsuspecting, arrives on the heath, the witches plan to torment a sea-captain whose wife has annoyed them.

2. *Killing swine:* Witches were said to kill farm animals, often in revenge for some supposed insult. There are still people who will buy unwanted articles from gipsy women because they fear a curse.

The Thane of Cawdor, began a dismal conflict,
Till that Bellona's bridegroom, lapp'd in proof,   55
Confronted him with self-comparisons,
Point against point rebellious, arm 'gainst arm,
Curbing his lavish spirit; and to conclude,
The victory fell on us.

Duncan   Great happiness!

Ross

That now   60
Sweno, the Norways' king, craves composition;
Nor would we deign him burial of his men
Till he disbursed, at Saint Colme's Inch,
Ten thousand dollars to our general use.

Duncan

No more that Thane of Cawdor shall deceive   65
Our bosom interest. Go pronounce his present death,
And with his former title greet Macbeth.

Ross

I'll see it done.

Duncan

What he hath lost, noble Macbeth hath won.

Exeunt

SCENE III—*A blasted heath*

Thunder.   Enter the three WITCHES

First Witch

Where hast thou been, sister?

Second Witch

Killing swine.

Third Witch

Sister, where thou?

First Witch

A sailor's wife had chestnuts in her lap,
And mounch'd, and mounch'd, and mounch'd.   5

7. *Aroint thee* . . . */* Get out!

rump-fed: this probably means 'fed on rump-steak', therefore sleek and plump. The gaunt witches would envy her.

ronyon: worthless woman.

8. *Tiger:* a common name for a ship in Shakespeare's time.

9. There are records of criminal trials in which so-called witches confessed that they went to sea in a sieve.

10. Another special ability of witches was to turn themselves into animals, but when they did this they were tailless and could be identified.

11. She seems almost incoherent with rage and malice. What do you think she intends to *do*?

15–18. *I myself have . . . card:* 'I have control of all the other winds and (I know) the exact harbours from which they blow, from all points of the compass card.' The main point is that she wants to keep the *Tiger* out of all ports, miserably tossing on the waves.

19. Because the *Tiger* will not be able to replenish her water-supply.

20–1. This is an ominous suggestion of Macbeth's later insomnia (see, for example, Act III, Scene iv, line 141).

21. *pent-house lid:* An eyelid slopes something like the roof of a penthouse. (A penthouse is a small structure built against a larger one, therefore having only one roof-slope).

22. *forbid:* cursed.

23. *sev'nights:* weeks. Compare the similar word fortnight (fourteen nights) which is still in regular use. The witch is going to manipulate the winds to keep the ship at sea for 81 weeks.

24. *dwindle, peak:* become thin.

25. *bark:* ship. It is important to note that the power of the witches is limited. At crucial points in the play Macbeth excuses himself by assuming that they have absolute power and knowledge, but this is not so.

29. *a pilot's thumb:* Bits of dead bodies were valued ingredients in making spells.

31. Is this perhaps a supernatural drum? There is no indication that Macbeth and Banquo have an escort, but they may have.

'Give me' quoth I.
'Aroint thee, witch!' the rump-fed ronyon cries.
Her husband's to Aleppo gone, master o' th' Tiger;
But in a sieve I'll thither sail
And, like a rat without a tail,   10
I'll do, I'll do, and I'll do.
Second Witch
  I'll give thee a wind.
First Witch
  Th'art kind.
Third Witch
  And I another.
First Witch
  I myself have all the other;   15
  And the very ports they blow,
  All the quarters that they know
  I' th' shipman's card.
  I'll drain him dry as hay:
  Sleep shall neither night nor day   20
  Hang upon his pent-house lid;
  He shall live a man forbid;
  Weary sev'nights, nine times nine,
  Shall he dwindle, peak, and pine.
  Though his bark cannot be lost,   25
  Yet it shall be tempest-tost.
  Look what I have.
Second Witch
  Show me, show me.
First Witch
  Here I have a pilot's thumb,
  Wreck'd as homeward he did come.   30

Drum within

Third Witch
  A drum, a drum!
  Macbeth doth come.

35

33. *Weird:* This comes from an Old English word 'wyrd', which means fate. The witches seem to claim some direct power of destiny, and Macbeth believes this, but (as noted above) they are servants of a greater power.

34. *Posters:* creatures which travel quickly.

35. *about, about:* The witches whirl round in a crazy dance.

36–7. Three and multiples of three have always been regarded as magic numbers. At this point they also indicate roughly the steps of their dance: 'three paces your way, three paces my way, and three more paces (in the direction of the Third Witch).'

38. *wound up:* 'set, and ready for action'. At this very moment Macbeth and Banquo enter, as though brought there by the charm.

39. *So foul and fair:* Macbeth's unconscious echo of the witches' words at Act I, Scene i, line 12 confirms the impression that he is already under their influence. He himself is referring to the desperate battle and its happy outcome for the Scots.

40. *How far is't call'd . . . ?* How far do they reckon it is . . . ?

40–62. Banquo's reaction to the first sight of the witches is a suspicious one. Are they earthly creatures or from hell? Can they be women, when they have beards? He can't place them. Macbeth says little, but seems far more prepared than Banquo to accept the witches' words.

43–4. *aught that man may question?* beings with whom one is permitted to communicate?

45. *choppy:* chapped. The fact that the witches put their fingers on their lips in answer to Banquo seems to suggest that they want to speak, not to him, but to Macbeth. What do you think Macbeth's attitude is at this moment?

49. *Glamis:* two syllables, in Shakespeare's time, but one nowadays. This title was already Macbeth's.

51. *hereafter:* in the future. They have just addressed him as the present Thane of Cawdor, as well as Glamis.

52. Banquo notices that Macbeth jumps when he hears the greetings, in a fearful way. Is this sufficiently accounted for by mere surprise and wonder, and the frightening appearance of the witches, or has Macbeth already considered the possibility of becoming king, by foul means if necessary?

54. *fantastical:* imaginary.

54–5. *or that . . . ye show?* or are you what you appear to be?

56–7. *present grace:* being Thane of Glamis.

great prediction Of noble having: becoming Thane of Cawdor.

royal hope: becoming king.

58. *rapt withal:* entranced by them (the witches' mysterious greetings).

59. *look into the seeds of time:* Banquo is prepared to grant the witches the power of seeing into the future, but he goes on at once (lines 61–2) to show that he will not put himself in their power. Their response is to speak to him in riddles, whereas they gave Macbeth plain statements.

36

All

    The Weird Sisters, hand in hand,
    Posters of the sea and land,
    Thus do go about, about;   *35*
    Thrice to thine, and thrice to mine,
    And thrice again, to make up nine.
    Peace! The charm's wound up.

           Enter MACBETH *and* BANQUO

Macbeth

    So foul and fair a day I have not seen.

Banquo

    How far is't call'd to Forres? What are these,   *40*
    So wither'd, and so wild in their attire,
    That look not like th' inhabitants o' th' earth,
    And yet are on't? Live you, or are you ought
    That man may question? You seem to understand me,
    By each at once her choppy finger laying   *45*
    Upon her skinny lips. You should be women,
    And yet your beards forbid me to interpret
    That you are so.

Macbeth   Speak, if you can. What are you?

First Witch

    All hail, Macbeth! Hail to thee, Thane of Glamis!

Second Witch

    All hail, Macbeth! Hail to thee, Thane of Cawdor!   *50*

Third Witch

    All hail, Macbeth, that shalt be King hereafter!

Banquo

    Good sir, why do you start, and seem to fear
    Things that do sound so fair? I' th' name of truth,
    Are ye fantastical, or that indeed
    Which outwardly ye show? My noble partner   *55*
    You greet with present grace and great prediction
    Of noble having and of royal hope,
    That he seems rapt withal. To me you speak not.
    If you can look into the seeds of time

68. *get kings:* be the ancestor of kings.

71. *imperfect speakers:* Macbeth says this because he wants to know more. He has come out of his trance and now demands further information.

72. *Sinel:* Macbeth's father, from whom he had inherited the title of Thane of Glamis.

73–4. Neither Macbeth nor Banquo seems to have heard of Cawdor's treachery.

75. *Stands not . . . belief:* Is so unlikely as to be unbelievable.

77. *owe:* own, possess.
intelligence: information.

79. Having asked for information twice Macbeth becomes bolder and orders the witches to answer him.

80–3. The witches have vanished like burst bubbles. Although they had seemed creatures of the material world, it now appears that they belong to the supernatural.

82. *corporal:* made of flesh and blood.

And say which grain will grow and which will not,   60
Speak then to me, who neither beg nor fear
Your favours nor your hate.
First Witch
    Hail!
Second Witch
    Hail!
Third Witch
    Hail!   65
First Witch
    Lesser than Macbeth, and greater.
Second Witch
    Not so happy, yet much happier.
Third Witch
    Thou shalt get kings, though thou be none.
    So, all hail, Macbeth and Banquo!
First Witch
    Banquo and Macbeth, all hail!   70
Macbeth
    Stay, you imperfect speakers, tell me more.
    By Sinel's death I know I am Thane of Glamis;
    But how of Cawdor? The Thane of Cawdor lives,
    A prosperous gentleman; and to be King
    Stands not within the prospect of belief,   75
    No more than to be Cawdor. Say from whence
    You owe this strange intelligence, or why
    Upon this blasted heath you stop our way
    With such prophetic greeting? Speak, I charge you.

WITCHES *vanish*

Banquo
    The earth hath bubbles, as the water has,   80
    And these are of them. Whither are they vanish'd?
Macbeth
    Into the air; and what seem'd corporal melted
    As breath into the wind. Would they had stay'd!

85–6. *the insane root . . . prisoner:* the root (of the hemlock or some other plant) which causes madness when eaten.

87. The first thing Macbeth mentions after the disappearance of the witches is a benefit they have conferred on Banquo. Is he envious and annoyed because no mention was made of his own heirs?

92. *Thy personal . . . fight:* Your individual contribution in putting down the rebellion of Macdonwald.

93–4. The king has two very strong feelings: his admiration of Macbeth's fighting qualities, and his wish to praise his general. He cannot find words to express his admiration. *Which should be thine or his* is a significant phrase. Might it also describe Macbeth's feelings at this time?

96. Ross goes on to mention the other phase of the battle, against the Norwegian forces.

stout: bold, tough.

97–8. *Nothing afeard . . . death:* Ross comments that Macbeth is not frightened by the sight of the mangled bodies of those he has killed. But there is more to it than this. *Images of death* are in the minds of the beholders. Before long Macbeth's own mind is full of such images, which appal him: the dead body of Duncan, Banquo's ghost, etc.

98–101. Macbeth's great achievement was acclaimed in all the messages which piled up in front of Duncan. There is a marked irony in the fact that, just when the audience has been given reason to suspect Macbeth, there is unanimous Scottish praise for the warrior-thane.

99. *post with post:* message after message.

103. *herald . . . sight:* escort you into the king's presence.

105. *for an earnest:* as a first instalment.

106–7. The words are close enough to those of the Second Witch to underline the rapid fulfilment of the prophecy.

addition: title.

108. Banquo has clearly decided that the witches are evil.

Banquo
　Were such things here as we do speak about?
　Or have we eaten on the insane root　　　　　　　*85*
　That takes the reason prisoner?
Macbeth
　Your children shall be kings.
Banquo　　　　　　　　　You shall be King.
Macbeth
　And Thane of Cawdor too; went it not so?
Banquo
　To th' self-same tune and words. Who's here?

　　　　　Enter ROSS *and* ANGUS

Ross
　The King hath happily receiv'd, Macbeth,　　　　*90*
　The news of thy success; and when he reads
　Thy personal venture in the rebels' fight,
　His wonders and his praises do contend
　Which should be thine or his. Silenc'd with that,
　In viewing o'er the rest o' th' self-same day,　　*95*
　He finds thee in the stout Norweyan ranks,
　Nothing afeard of what thyself didst make,
　Strange images of death. As thick as tale
　Came post with post, and every one did bear
　Thy praises in his kingdom's great defence,　　*100*
　And pour'd them down before him.
Angus　　　　　　　　　　We are sent
　To give thee, from our royal master, thanks;
　Only to herald thee into his sight,
　Not pay thee.
Ross
　And, for an earnest of a greater honour,　　　　*105*
　He bade me, from him, call thee Thane of Cawdor;
　In which addition, hail, most worthy Thane!
　For it is thine.
Banquo　　　　　What, can the devil speak true?

109–10. It has often been noticed that the play contains many examples of imagery derived from clothes, particularly clothes that do not fit. One of the effects is to build up a picture of Macbeth as a man wearing clothes that were not tailored for him. Keep this in mind as the play develops.

111–12. The ex-thane of Cawdor is under sentence of death (see Act I, Scene ii, line 66).

was combin'd: allied himself.

113. *line the rebel:* assist Macdonwald.

114. *hidden help and vantage:* secret aid.

115. *labour'd . . . wreck:* strove to ruin his country.

116. *treasons capital:* acts of treason worthy of the death penalty.

118. *The greatest is behind:* the fulfilment of the Third Witch's prophecy, the Kingship, remains in the future.

119. Macbeth again refers to the prophecy about Banquo's children becoming kings.

121. *trusted home:* believed in fully.

122. *Might yet . . . crown:* Might make you burn with hope of becoming king.

123–7. Banquo, after a few words of what seems to be straightforward encouragement of Macbeth, again reveals his own deep distrust of the witches and their words.

124–7. The agents of the Devil often impress us and win our confidence with a few small truths so that, once we are in their power, they can deceive us in really important matters (and thus destroy us).

129–30. *the swelling act . . . theme:* Macbeth sees himself as king at the climax of a great drama. After a brief acknowledgement of the outside world in line 130 (*I thank you, gentlemen*) he sinks again into his musing on the witches' words.

131. *soliciting:* prompting, egging on.

132–4. What Banquo suspected and dismissed (a small truth leading to betrayal *In deepest consequence*) Macbeth also suspects but will not dismiss.

135–8. *If good . . . nature?* Already Macbeth is contradicting Ross's remark in lines 97–8. Here is an *image of death* of which he is clearly afraid. Is it one of his own creation or not? He is certainly contemplating the possibility of murder (see line 140).

136. *unfix my hair:* make my hair stand on end.

137. *seated:* firmly fixed.

138. *Against the use of nature:* in an unnatural way.

138–9. *Present fears . . . imaginings:* A real cause of fear (e.g. a fierce enemy in the recent battle) is less frightening than something horrible conjured up in the imagination.

Macbeth
  The Thane of Cawdor lives; why do you dress me
  In borrow'd robes?
Angus   Who was the Thane lives yet;   110
  But under heavy judgment bears that life
  Which he deserves to lose. Whether he was combin'd
  With those of Norway, or did line the rebel
  With hidden help and vantage, or that with both
  He labour'd in his country's wreck, I know not;   115
  But treasons capital, confess'd and prov'd,
  Have overthrown him.
Macbeth [*aside*]   Glamis, and Thane of Cawdor!
  The greatest is behind.—Thanks for your pains.
  [*Aside to* BANQUO] Do you not hope your children
      shall be kings,
  When those that gave the Thane of Cawdor to me   120
  Promis'd no less to them?
Banquo [*aside to* MACBETH]   That, trusted home,
  Might yet enkindle you unto the crown,
  Besides the Thane of Cawdor. But 'tis strange;
  And oftentimes to win us to our harm,
  The instruments of darkness tell us truths,   125
  Win us with honest trifles, to betray's
  In deepest consequence.—
  Cousins, a word, I pray you.
Macbeth [*aside*]   Two truths are told,
  As happy prologues to the swelling act
  Of the imperial theme.—I thank you, gentlemen.   130
  [*Aside*] This supernatural soliciting
  Cannot be ill; cannot be good. If ill,
  Why hath it given me earnest of success,
  Commencing in a truth? I am Thane of Cawdor.
  If good, why do I yield to that suggestion   135
  Whose horrid image doth unfix my hair
  And make my seated heart knock at my ribs
  Against the use of nature? Present fears
  Are less than horrible imaginings.

140–3. Macbeth is obsessed by the idea of murder and is incapable of normal action. Nothing seems real to him except what he is creating in his mind.

144. *rapt:* lost in his own thoughts.

145–6. Macbeth adopts a fatalistic attitude, to escape his *horrible imaginings.* 'Why, there is no need for me to take any action; if it is my destiny to be king, it will just happen that way.'

146–7. *New honours . . . use:* The honours which have just come to him (Macbeth) are like new clothes which take time to shape themselves comfortably to the body.

148–9. *Come what . . . roughest day:* Macbeth continues to shrug off his troubled thoughts; 'I suppose I shall live through it. Even the most troubled day has to come to an end.' The words give him something to hang on to.
150. Banquo indicates politely that they are waiting until Macbeth is ready to go.

151–2. 'Do forgive me. My over-tired brain was disturbed by things that I can't even remember now'. A simple untruth, but worth noting.
152–4. Macbeth has a talent for polite expression that sometimes degenerates into wordy humbug. Here he may be more or less sincere, but the same kind of phrase is later used for deceitful purposes (see, for example, the beginning of Act III, Scene iv, the Banquet Scene).
152. *your pains:* your services to me.
153–4. *where every day . . . read them:* i.e. in his mind.

156. *The interim having weigh'd it:* the interval having given us a chance to consider it.
157. *Our free hearts:* Can either of their hearts be described as *free*?

My thought, whose murder yet is but fantastical,   *140*
Shakes so my single state of man
That function is smother'd in surmise,
And nothing is but what is not.
Banquo
    Look how our partner's rapt.
Macbeth [aside]
    If chance will have me King, why, chance may crown
        me,   *145*
    Without my stir.
Banquo   New honours come upon him,
    Like our strange garments, cleave not to their mould
    But with the aid of use.
Macbeth [aside]   Come what come may,
    Time and the hour runs through the roughest day.
Banquo
    Worthy Macbeth, we stay upon your leisure.   *150*
Macbeth
    Give me your favour. My dull brain was wrought
    With things forgotten. Kind gentlemen, your pains
    Are register'd where every day I turn
    The leaf to read them. Let us toward the King.
    [*Aside to* BANQUO] Think upon what hath chanc'd; and,
        at more time,   *155*
    The interim having weigh'd it, let us speak
    Our free hearts each to other.
Banquo [aside to MACBETH]*   Very gladly.
Macbeth [aside to BANQUO]*
    Till then, enough.—Come, friends.

Exeunt

MACBETH

SCENE IV

Now that the rebels and the foreign invaders have been defeated, King Duncan wants to celebrate and confirm the new stability of the state by appointing Malcolm, his eldest son, as the official heir to the throne. It is a formal occasion, which would have been vividly presented by Shakespeare's company, the King's Men, with rich costume and all the symbols of majesty. The words of the scene stress happy, natural relationships in family and society, with Duncan as the warm-hearted father-king. Macbeth's apparently unexpected arrival gives Duncan further opportunity for rejoicing.

2. *Those in commission:* 'the officials charged with the duty' (Ross was sent to deal with it, Act 1, Scene ii, lines 66–7).

9. *As one . . . death:* Like an actor perfectly trained in a death-scene. *studied:* learnt by heart.
10. *the dearest thing he ow'd:* his life.
ow'd: owned.
11. *careless:* not worth any care.
11–12. *There's no art . . . face:* 'There's no way of telling, from a man's face, what's going on in his mind'. At this moment Macbeth enters and the innocent-minded Duncan has no idea that his own words could be accurately applied to his new Thane of Cawdor. This is a good example of dramatic irony.

16–18. *Thou art . . . overtake thee:* You are so far ahead in worth and ability that it's difficult for recognition and reward to catch up with you.

19–20. *That the proportion . . . mine!* So that I could have thanked you and rewarded you according to your merit.

22–3. *The service . . . itself:* Macbeth is not saying much more than 'I was only doing my duty'. In this speech and in others at important moments he is wordy and insincere. Is this a sign of guilt or embarrassment?
24–7. *our duties . . . honour:* Macbeth's comments indicate an awareness of the value of stable relationships in family and state – relationships which he is soon to shatter brutally.

SCENE IV—*Forres.*   *The palace*

   Flourish.   *Enter* DUNCAN, MALCOLM, DONALBAIN,
       LENNOX *and* ATTENDANTS

Duncan
  Is execution done on Cawdor? Are not
  Those in commission yet return'd?
Malcolm   My liege,
  They are not yet come back. But I have spoke
  With one that saw him die; who did report
  That very frankly he confess'd his treasons,   5
  Implor'd your Highness' pardon, and set forth
  A deep repentance. Nothing in his life
  Became him like the leaving it: he died
  As one that had been studied in his death
  To throw away the dearest thing he ow'd   10
  As 'twere a careless trifle.
Duncan   There's no art
  To find the mind's construction in the face.
  He was a gentleman on whom I built
  An absolute trust.

     Enter MACBETH, BANQUO, ROSS *and* ANGUS

         O worthiest cousin!
  The sin of my ingratitude even now   15
  Was heavy on me. Thou art so far before
  That swiftest wing of recompense is slow
  To overtake thee. Would thou hadst less deserv'd,
  That the proportion both of thanks and payment
  Might have been mine! Only I have left to say,   20
  More is thy due than more than all can pay.
Macbeth
  The service and the loyalty I owe,
  In doing it, pays itself. Your Highness' part
  Is to receive our duties; and our duties
  Are to your throne and state children and servants, 25

27. *Safe toward . . . honour:* with a sure respect to you, in love and honour.

28–9. *I have . . . growing:* Duncan uses natural imagery to express his spontaneous, warm personality and, in lines 32–3, Banquo's response is in similar terms. Macbeth, on the other hand, is already considering highly unnatural courses.

34. *Wanton:* unrestrained.
34–5. *seek . . . sorrow:* (my joyful feelings) disguise themselves in tears, which usually express sorrow.

37. *We:* Duncan now speaks formally, as king.
37–9. The throne of Scotland was not hereditary. The king was entitled to appoint his successor from among his relatives (Macbeth was eligible, among others) and usually made him Prince of Cumberland at the same time. This was the recognized title of the heir to the throne, just as Prince of Wales is of the heir to the throne of Great Britain today.
39–42. *which honour . . . deservers:* My son's new title will not be the only honour to be conferred; everyone who deserves recognition will receive it.
42. *From hence to Inverness:* Duncan turns to Macbeth, who is to be his host at Inverness.
43. *bind us further to you:* Duncan indicates again that he is already deeply indebted to Macbeth for his bravery and success in battle; now he is to be indebted to him as his guest.
44. *The rest . . . you:* A rather strained piece of politeness; 'any time or trouble not spent in serving you is hard work'.
45. *harbinger:* a man who rode ahead to make arrangements for accommodation for an army or a royal company.

48–53. The recognition of Malcolm as heir to the throne is a serious obstacle to Macbeth's now acknowledged ambition. His response is to commit himself to evil action. Again, Macbeth's words show that he knows only too well how evil his desires are. They are *black* and *deep* and fit only for the darkest night.

52–3. *The eye . . . to see:* Let my eye be blind to what my hand does, but let the deed be done, even though the murdered body is too horrible to look at.

Which do but what they should by doing everything
Safe toward your love and honour.

Duncan   Welcome hither.
I have begun to plant thee, and will labour
To make thee full of growing. Noble Banquo,
That hast no less deserv'd, nor must be known   *30*
No less to have done so, let me infold thee
And hold thee to my heart.

Banquo   There if I grow,
The harvest is your own.

Duncan   My plenteous joys,
Wanton in fulness, seek to hide themselves
In drops of sorrow. Sons, kinsmen, thanes,   *35*
And you whose places are the nearest, know
We will establish our estate upon
Our eldest, Malcolm, whom we name hereafter
The Prince of Cumberland; which honour must
Not unaccompanied invest him only,   *40*
But signs of nobleness, like stars, shall shine
On all deservers. From hence to Inverness,
And bind us further to you.

Macbeth
The rest is labour, which is not us'd for you.
I'll be myself the harbinger, and make joyful   *45*
The hearing of my wife with your approach;
So, humbly take my leave.

Duncan   My worthy Cawdor!

Macbeth [aside]
The Prince of Cumberland! That is a step,
On which I must fall down, or else o'er-leap,
For in my way it lies. Stars, hide your fires;   *50*
Let not light see my black and deep desires.
The eye wink at the hand; yet let that be
Which the eye fears, when it is done, to see.

                    Exit

49

54. While Macbeth has been soliloquizing (probably at the front of the stage), Banquo has been praising him to Duncan.
55–6. *And in . . . to me:* Hearing him praised gives me as much satisfaction as a fine meal eaten with ceremony and in good company.

58. *peerless:* unequalled.
Some critics have called Duncan a weak king. Can you justify or refute this from the evidence we have up to this point?

SCENE V

Macbeth's last words in the previous scene expressed firm, if horrified, resolve. His letter to his wife is confident. Her reaction to it is fierce and eager. She sees that Macbeth's better feelings (*human kindness*) will stand in the way of ambition; she plans to overcome them. First she has to cope with the gentler side of her own nature, and does so in a terrible appeal to the forces of evil. When Macbeth enters he is non-committal.

1. When Lady Macbeth begins to speak she is halfway through the reading of the letter. There is no mention of the witches' promises to Banquo in the part we hear.
2–3. *by the perfect'st report . . . knowledge:* It sounds as though Macbeth is referring to the proved truth of the Cawdor prophecy.
6. *missives:* messengers.

10. *to deliver thee:* to pass on to you.

11–12. *the dues of rejoicing:* your fair share of joy.

13. *Lay it to thy heart:* 'consider well what I have written'. But she probably also takes the words literally by hiding the letter in her bosom.
14–15. *shalt be . . . promis'd:* Lady Macbeth begins with a flat statement that her husband shall become king.

17. *To catch the nearest way:* to take the shortest route (to what you want).
19. *The illness should attend it:* the evil which must be the partner of Macbeth's ambition.
19–20. *What thou . . . holily:* You would like to attain your great ambition without doing anything wrong.
21. *wrongly win:* gain what you are not entitled to.
22. *Thou'dst have:* You want.
22–3. *that which cries . . . have it:* the thing (i.e. the crown) which cries 'You must do the murder' if you want it.

wrong

Duncan

True, worthy Banquo: he is full so valiant;
And in his commendations I am fed;
It is a banquet to me. Let's after him,   *55*
Whose care is gone before to bid us welcome.
It is a peerless kinsman.

Flourish   Exeunt

SCENE V—*Inverness.   Macbeth's castle*

Enter LADY MACBETH, *reading a letter*

Lady Macbeth

'They met me in the day of success; and I have
learn'd by the perfect'st report they have more in
them than mortal knowledge. When I burn'd in desire
to question them further, they made themselves air,
into which they vanish'd. Whiles I stood rapt in the   *5*
wonder of it, came missives from the King, who all-
hail'd me "Thane of Cawdor"; by which title, before,
these weird sisters saluted me, and referr'd me to the
coming on of time, with "Hail, king that shalt be!"
This have I thought good to deliver thee, my dearest   *10*
partner of greatness, that thou mightst not lose the
dues of rejoicing by being ignorant of what greatness
is promis'd thee. Lay it to thy heart, and farewell.'
Glamis thou art, and Cawdor; and shalt be
What thou art promis'd. Yet do I fear thy nature;   *15*
It is too full o' th' milk of human kindness
To catch the nearest way. Thou wouldst be great;
Art not without ambition, but without
The illness should attend it. What thou wouldst highly,
That wouldst thou holily; wouldst not play false,   *20*
And yet wouldst wrongly win.
Thou'dst have, great Glamis, that which cries
'Thus thou must do' if thou have it;

24-5. Lady Macbeth knows that Macbeth wishes Duncan to be murdered but that he himself will hesitate to do it.

25. *Hie thee hither:* hurry here.

25-30. The contemplated crime, which has already begun to destroy Macbeth's character, is having an equally destructive effect on his wife. All her aggressive, unfeminine instincts are being encouraged, and in lines 40-54 she makes a conscious request that her tender, womanly qualities should be taken away.

28. *the golden round:* the crown.

29. *fate and metaphysical aid:* Both powers (fate and the supernatural) are combined in the witches (see note to Act I, Scene iii, line 33).

31. The news of the king's impending arrival plays into her hands so astonishingly that she is taken off her guard.

33. *Would ... preparation:* Would have let me know so that I could get things ready.

35. *had the speed of him:* was able to ride faster.

36-7. *had scarcely more ... message:* gave his news with what was almost his last breath.

37. *Give him tending:* Look after him (i.e. get him refreshment, etc.).

38-40. *The raven ... battlements:* The raven, an ominous bird, with a harsh croaking cry, is even more hoarse than usual. Lady Macbeth, as well as her husband, is acutely aware of the enormity of the crime they are going to commit, but, unlike him, she does not hesitate for a moment. Notice that she says *my battlements*. She has taken over from her husband, in some respects, already.

40-1. *spirits ... thoughts:* the spirits which deal with murderous and destructive ideas in human minds.

41. *unsex me here:* She appeals to the powers of evil to take away her feminine qualities and to replace them with *direst cruelty*. This is certainly horrible, but it is important to note that it implies that she begins by being feminine and having tender feelings. Also, it is clear that she does not succeed in repressing her womanly nature completely; later (see Act V, Scene i) when she has a nervous breakdown she is very much a broken woman, and not an evil monster.

43-4. *Make thick ... remorse:* thicken my blood so that pity and sorrow cannot flow through my veins (and soften my heart).

45. *compunctious visitings of nature:* pangs of conscience.

46. *fell:* deadly.

46-7. *keep peace ... and it:* restrain me from putting my purpose into effect.

48. *take my milk for gall:* 'change my milk into gall' (an intensely bitter substance).

49. *sightless:* invisible.

50. *You wait ... mischief:* (wherever) you direct your evil influences in the sphere of nature.

50-4. There is a remarkable similarity between this part of her 'prayer' and Macbeth's *Stars, hide your fires* (Act 1, Scene iv, lines 50-3). She is, as it were, forestalling Heaven. She welcomes night and darkness much more eagerly and with much greater determination than her husband. Notice that she again uses the word *my*; this time it is *my keen knife*, as though she intends to commit the murder herself.

And that which rather thou dost fear to do
Than wishest should be undone. Hie thee hither,   25
That I may pour my spirits in thine ear,
And chastise with the valour of my tongue
All that impedes thee from the golden round
Which fate and metaphysical aid doth seem
To have thee crown'd withal.

Enter a MESSENGER

What is your tidings ? *30*

Messenger
The King comes here to-night.
Lady Macbeth   Thou'rt mad to say it.
Is not thy master with him ? who, were't so,
Would have inform'd for preparation.
Messenger
So please you, it is true. Our Thane is coming.
One of my fellows had the speed of him,   35
Who, almost dead for breath, had scarcely more
Than would make up his message.
Lady Macbeth   Give him tending:
He brings great news.

Exit MESSENGER

The raven himself is hoarse
That croaks the fatal entrance of Duncan
Under my battlements. Come, you spirits   40
That tend on mortal thoughts, unsex me here;
And fill me, from the crown to the toe, top-full
Of direst cruelty. Make thick my blood,
Stop up th' access and passage to remorse,
That no compunctious visitings of nature   45
Shake my fell purpose nor keep peace between
Th' effect and it. Come to my woman's breasts,
And take my milk for gall, you murd'ring ministers,
Wherever in your sightless substances
You wait on nature's mischief. Come, thick night,   50

MACBETH

51. *pall thee:* shroud yourself.
dunnest: darkest.

54. *Hold:* Stop.

55. *the all-hail hereafter:* The close echo of the Third Witch's words almost identifies her with the witch.

57. *This ignorant present:* the present which knows nothing of the future.
57–8. *I feel now . . . instant:* She stresses that the deed is as good as done, the crown virtually gained already. Macbeth does not respond to this, although he must understand it. Note the contrast between Lady Macbeth's eager confidence and Macbeth's uncertainty or reluctance.

60–1. *O, never Shall . . . morrow see:* She says emphatically that the next morning will not see Duncan departing. There is also a hint of omnipotence about the words, as though she and Macbeth between them could stop the sun rising. Ross's account of the wild weather of the following morning (Act II, Scene iv, lines 5–10) shows that there is something unintentionally prophetic in her words.
63. *beguile the time:* 'deceive everyone' (i.e. those present on the occasion).
64. *Look like the time:* put on an expression which suits the occasion.

66–8. There is dreadful, almost leering ambiguity about phrases like *provided for* and *This night's great business* or perhaps these euphemisms for 'murdered' and 'murder' may be signs that Lady Macbeth is not as ruthless as she would wish.
67. *into my dispatch:* 'Leave it all to me' she says, but she also puns on the word *dispatch*, which means both 'management' and 'killing'. There are many examples of playing with words in *Macbeth*, some subtle, some more obvious; none of them would have raised laughter in Shakespeare's original audiences, but a kind of fascinated horror, accentuated by appreciation of the verbal skill.
69–70. (Tonight's events) will give us absolute power for the rest of our lives.
71. Macbeth does not share her confidence in the outcome, and cannot look her in the eye, as her next remark shows.
72. To change one's expression always reveals fear (and suspicion is aroused).

And pall thee in the dunnest smoke of hell,
That my keen knife see not the wound it makes,
Nor heaven peep through the blanket of the dark
To cry 'Hold, hold'.

Enter MACBETH

         Great Glamis! Worthy Cawdor!
Greater than both, by the all-hail hereafter!   55
Thy letters have transported me beyond
This ignorant present, and I feel now
The future in the instant.
Macbeth   My dearest love,
Duncan comes here to-night.
Lady Macbeth   And when goes hence?
Macbeth
To-morrow—as he purposes.
Lady Macbeth   O, never   60
Shall sun that morrow see!
Your face, my thane, is as a book where men
May read strange matters. To beguile the time,
Look like the time; bear welcome in your eye,
Your hand, your tongue; look like th' innocent
    flower,   65
But be the serpent under't. He that's coming
Must be provided for; and you shall put
This night's great business into my dispatch;
Which shall to all our nights and days to come
Give solely sovereign sway and masterdom.   70
Macbeth
We will speak further.
Lady Macbeth   Only look up clear.
To alter favour ever is to fear.
Leave all the rest to me.

Exeunt

SCENE VI

There is a dreadful irony about this scene, with the innocent king delighting in the appearance of the Macbeths' castle and in what he sees as the generous hospitality of the Macbeths themselves. Lady Macbeth seems almost to overdo her humble greeting (lines 14–20) but the king suspects nothing. Do you see him as naive or even senile in his innocence?

Stage Direction *Hautboys:* oboes.

torches: These were normally used on the Elizabethan stage only to indicate night-scenes, but it is about sunset and the attendants have come out of a darkening castle interior, which is particularly symbolic of what has been plotted there.

1. *seat:* situation.

3. *gentle senses:* Perhaps Duncan means that his senses have become less acute with age; in any case the word helps to build up our impression of him.

guest of summer: migrant bird, summer visitor.

4. *martlet:* This is almost certainly the house-martin, and not the swift (which is its modern meaning). Banquo suggests that it prefers to build its nest on church walls.

approve: show.

5. *By his lov'd mansionry:* by the fact that it chooses the castle for its home-building.

5–6. *the heaven's breath . . . here:* the breezes are soft and attractive here.

jutty: projecting part of the building.

7. *coign of vantage:* Dr Johnson suggested that this means 'convenient corner'.

8. *pendent bed and procreant cradle:* the hanging nests in which the birds produce their young.

10. *delicate:* soft and sweet.

11–14. Duncan seems to be saying something like this: 'I am sometimes bothered by the love my attendants show me (perhaps because he is such a modest man) but I always acknowledge it. You should pray God to reward me for the trouble I am causing you'.

14–20. Lady Macbeth returns Duncan's compliment very prettily. We know she is insincere, but we must recognize her talent. Briefly, she is saying that, even if her efforts were quadrupled, they would not measure up to the honour the king is bestowing on her.

We rest your hermits: 'We will always pray for you' (like a religious recluse).

22. *purveyor:* one who went on ahead of a king to prepare accommodation for him.

23. *holp:* helped.

SCENE VI—*Inverness.   Before Macbeth's castle*

Hautboys and torches. Enter DUNCAN, MALCOLM,
DONALBAIN, BANQUO, LENNOX, MACDUFF, ROSS,
ANGUS *and* ATTENDANTS

Duncan
 This castle hath a pleasant seat; the air
 Nimbly and sweetly recommends itself
 Unto our gentle senses.
Banquo   This guest of summer,
 The temple-haunting martlet, does approve
 By his lov'd mansionry that the heaven's breath   5
 Smells wooingly here; no jutty, frieze,
 Buttress, nor coign of vantage, but this bird
 Hath made her pendent bed and procreant cradle.
 Where they most breed and haunt, I have observ'd
 The air is delicate.

Enter LADY MACBETH

Duncan   See, see, our honour'd hostess! 10
 The love that follows us sometime is our trouble,
 Which still we thank as love. Herein I teach you
 How you shall bid God 'ield us for your pains,
 And thank us for your trouble.
Lady Macbeth   All our service
 In every point twice done, and then done double, 15
 Were poor and single business to contend
 Against those honours deep and broad wherewith
 Your Majesty loads our house; for those of old,
 And the late dignities heap'd up to them,
 We rest your hermits.
Duncan   Where's the Thane of Cawdor? 20
 We cours'd him at the heels and had a purpose
 To be his purveyor; but he rides well,
 And his great love, sharp as his spur, hath holp him
 To his home before us. Fair and noble hostess,

25–8. Your servants always have their servants, themselves and everything that belongs to them ready to please your Highness, and to offer to him what is really his already.

31. *By your leave:* He is really repeating that he wants to take her hand, or else he kisses her on the cheek.

SCENE VII

In this scene Macbeth clearly and fully argues the case against murdering Duncan, and decides against it. The force of Lady Macbeth's scorn and eloquence changes his mind again; her determination and confidence brush aside his fears and scruples.

Stage Direction *Sewer:* This word originally meant the servant who tasted the food of a prominent person to make sure that it was not poisoned. Here it seems to refer to the man who superintends the laying of the banquet table.

1–28. This speech has often been regarded as one of the great Shakespearian 'set-piece' soliloquies (remember that Shakespeare uses such speeches to give his characters the opportunity for self-revelation). Macbeth begins uneasily arguing with himself, perhaps almost muttering, but later he becomes deeply moved and eloquent. It is useful, and often satisfying, to try such speeches out for oneself.

1. The first *done* means 'over and done with'.

2–3. *If th'assassination . . . consequence:* if the murder could be completely decisive and without unpleasant results.

trammel: entangle in a net.

4. *surcease:* death.

5. *here:* on earth.

6. *this bank and shoal of time:* Macbeth seems to view human life as a sandbank in eternity. Many of his actions do seem to be based on the idea that he is in a predicament like a shipwreck.

7. *We'd jump the life to come:* I'd risk what comes after death.

8–10. Macbeth is worried that a bloody act often provokes bloody retaliation.

10–12. *This even-handed justice . . . lips:* Impartial justice rules that we should drink the poison we administer to another.

12–28. Macbeth now speaks with real emotion, and in doing so reveals a genuine respect for Duncan's goodness, and also a respect for decent human values. He knows, clearly, that what he is thinking of doing is evil.

12–16. The *double trust* is (*a*) the combined relationship of being a relative and a subject, and (*b*) being the king's host.

17. *Hath borne . . . meek:* Has used his authority as king with such genuine humility.

18. *clear:* innocent.

We are your guest to-night.
Lady Macbeth   Your servants ever
Have theirs, themselves, and what is theirs, in compt,
To make their audit at your Highness' pleasure,
Still to return your own.
Duncan   Give me your hand;
Conduct me to mine host. We love him highly,
And shall continue our graces towards him.   3
By your leave, hostess.

Exeunt

SCENE VII—*Inverness.   Macbeth's castle*

Hautboys, torches.   Enter a SEWER, *and divers* SER-
VANTS *with dishes and service over the stage.   Then
enter* MACBETH

Macbeth
If it were done when 'tis done, then 'twere well
It were done quickly. If th' assassination
Could trammel up the consequence, and catch,
With his surcease, success; that but this blow
Might be the be-all and the end-all here—   5
But here upon this bank and shoal of time—
We'd jump the life to come. But in these cases
We still have judgment here, that we but teach
Bloody instructions, which being taught return
To plague th' inventor. This even-handed justice   10
Commends th' ingredience of our poison'd chalice
To our own lips. He's here in double trust:
First, as I am his kinsman and his subject—
Strong both against the deed; then, as his host,
Who should against his murderer shut the door,   15
Not bear the knife myself. Besides, this Duncan
Hath borne his faculties so meek, hath been
So clear in his great office, that his virtues

20. *taking-off:* murder.

21–5. The two pictures, of the baby and the *cherubin*, would not have seemed as similar to Shakespeare's audience as they do to us. Cherubs were not chubby babies but senior angels. But both baby and angels are riding the winds (*blast* and *sightless couriers* or invisible runners) and they are all, in Macbeth's vivid imagination, going to make the crime known to all (*blow the horrid deed in every eye*).

27–8. Jumping directly into one's saddle was a young man's way of showing-off. Possibly Shakespeare means 'overshoots and falls to the ground on the other side' by the last few words. Or it could mean simply that the rider, having cleared an obstacle, falls off his horse on the other side of it. In any case it is clear that Macbeth now knows that this ambition is an evil one.

29. This is the first of several occasions when Lady Macbeth sharply questions her husband on his actions. Note the others as they occur.

31. Macbeth's statement sounds decisive, and it certainly follows on logically from his recent argument with himself, but it does not take Lady Macbeth very long to shake his resolution.

32–5. It is interesting that Macbeth does not mention to his wife the objections to the murder that appear to carry most weight with him – the moral and ethical objections. To her he merely talks about ruining his reputation (*Golden opinions*). Although they are in many ways so close, would it be true to say that they rarely communicate on the deepest level? This is a question you might attempt to answer when you have finished the play.

34. *in their newest gloss:* like fresh, new clothes, perfectly clean.

35–7. Lady Macbeth takes up Macbeth's metaphor from clothing and mixes it with one from drunkenness. She goes on to suggest that Macbeth is like someone waking up with a hang-over (*green and pale*) who forgets or ignores what he had decided to do when he was drunk.

39–41. *Art thou afeard . . . in desire?* Are you afraid to put firmly into practice what you really want to do?

39–45. She uses two very powerful (and unfair) weapons here. She says 'I see you don't really love me' (*From this time Such I account thy love*) and accuses him of being a coward. Macbeth has no defence against such tactics.

42. Lady Macbeth takes it for granted that her husband's *ornament of life* would be the crown of Scotland, a very different prize from the *eternal jewel* he regrets the loss of later (Act III, Scene i, line 66).

45. *th' adage:* the proverb. Lady Macbeth is referring to 'The cat would eat fish, and would not wet her feet'. The ridiculousness of the comparison between Macbeth and the cat seems to affect him deeply because he asks her to be quiet.

Will plead like angels, trumpet-tongu'd, against
The deep damnation of his taking-off;   *20*
And pity, like a naked new-born babe,
Striding the blast, or heaven's cherubin hors'd
Upon the sightless couriers of the air,
Shall blow the horrid deed in every eye,
That tears shall drown the wind. I have no spur   *25*
To prick the sides of my intent, but only
Vaulting ambition, which o'er-leaps itself,
And falls on th' other.

Enter LADY MACBETH

How now! What news?

Lady Macbeth
He has almost supp'd. Why have you left the chamber?
Macbeth
Hath he ask'd for me?
Lady Macbeth   Know you not he has?   *30*
Macbeth
We will proceed no further in this business.
He hath honour'd me of late; and I have bought
Golden opinions from all sorts of people,
Which would be worn now in their newest gloss,
Not cast aside so soon.
Lady Macbeth   Was the hope drunk   *35*
Wherein you dress'd yourself? Hath it slept since,
And wakes it now to look so green and pale
At what it did so freely? From this time
Such I account thy love. Art thou afeard
To be the same in thine own act and valour   *40*
As thou art in desire? Wouldst thou have that
Which thou esteem'st the ornament of life,
And live a coward in thine own esteem,
Letting 'I dare not' wait upon 'I would',
Like the poor cat i' th' adage?
Macbeth   Prithee, peace;   *45*
I dare do all that may become a man;

47–8. *What beast was't then . . . to me?* Does this suggest that they have discussed the murder 'off-stage', i.e. in a scene that Shakespeare has not written for us? Or was Macbeth's letter to his wife a clear enough reference to the *enterprise*?

50–1. *And to be more . . . the man:* You would be even more brave and manly if you made yourself king, rather than just a thane.
51–4. *Nor . . . you:* When there was no opportunity, you wished to create one; when the opportunity presents itself, you are afraid to take it.

54–9. Lady Macbeth has seen the effect of her taunts on her husband and now comes out with the most outrageous and shocking statement of all. It sounds as though the *murd'ring ministers* she appealed to (Act I, Scene v, lines 47–8) have done as she asked; yet the force of these words depends on her and her husband's awareness that they are horrible and unnatural. In reply all Macbeth can say is, feebly, *If we should fail?*

60. *We fail!* How do you think she says these words – realistically ('Well, then, we fail') or scornfully ('How could we possibly fail?')?

64. *chamberlains:* officials of the royal bedchamber.

65. *wine and wassail:* drink and revelry. It almost sounds as though Lady Macbeth intends to urge them on to cheerful drunkenness herself, but probably she proposes simply to give them plenty of drink, with the encouragement to feel free to indulge themselves.
66–8. *That memory . . . only:* Memory, the keeper of one part of the brain, will be turned into smoke by the drink, which will smother the rest of the brain, where the rational faculty usually operates.
68. *limbec:* alembic, a kind of retort.
69. *drenched:* drowned – but a 'drench' is animal medicine (e.g. poured down a horse's throat from a bottle) and something of this meaning is also conveyed.
72. *spongy:* drunken.
73. *quell:* murder (the word comes from the same origin as 'kill').
73–5. What mixture of emotions do you sense in Macbeth's words?
74. *mettle:* spirit, temperament.
75. *receiv'd:* accepted.

Who dares do more is none.
Lady Macbeth   What beast was't then
That made you break this enterprise to me?
When you durst do it, then you were a man;
And to be more than what you were, you would   50
Be so much more the man. Nor time nor place
Did then adhere, and yet you would make both;
They have made themselves, and that their fitness now
Does unmake you. I have given suck, and know
How tender 'tis to love the babe that milks me—   55
I would, while it was smiling in my face,
Have pluck'd my nipple from his boneless gums,
And dash'd the brains out, had I so sworn
As you have done to this.
Macbeth   If we should fail?
Lady Macbeth
We fail!   60
But screw your courage to the sticking place,
And we'll not fail. When Duncan is asleep—
Whereto the rather shall his day's hard journey
Soundly invite him—his two chamberlains
Will I with wine and wassail so convince   65
That memory, the warder of the brain,
Shall be a fume, and the receipt of reason
A limbec only. When in swinish sleep
Their drenched natures lie as in a death,
What cannot you and I perform upon   70
Th' unguarded Duncan? what not put upon
His spongy officers, who shall bear the guilt
Of our great quell?
Macbeth   Bring forth men-children only;
For thy undaunted mettle should compose
Nothing but males. Will it not be receiv'd,   75
When we have mark'd with blood those sleepy two
Of his own chamber, and us'd their very daggers,
That they have done't?
Lady Macbeth   Who dares receive it other,

79. When the time comes Macbeth certainly does make his *griefs and clamour roar* – even to excess. As far as Duncan's murder is concerned he is now entirely in his wife's hands and takes her whole plan very literally.

80. *bend up:* i.e. like a man preparing a crossbow for firing.

81. *Each corporal agent:* All my physical powers.

82–3. Although now *settled*, Macbeth remains fully aware of the deceit and wickedness involved, whereas, at times, his wife seems to be able to delude herself into a sense of glory in the deed (e.g. line 73, *great quell*. Macbeth calls it a *deep damnation* in line 20, and a *terrible feat* in line 81).

As we shall make our griefs and clamour roar
Upon his death?
Macbeth   I am settled, and bend up   *80*
Each corporal agent to this terrible feat.
Away, and mock the time with fairest show;
False face must hide what the false heart doth know.

Exeunt

ACT TWO

SCENE I

Apart from furthering the action, and creating the atmosphere of horror before the murder, this scene also shows the difference between Banquo and Macbeth as men. Banquo and his son Fleance are good companions, and Banquo, afflicted with *cursed thoughts*, appeals to the *Merciful powers* of goodness for aid in fighting them. He also makes it fairly clear just afterwards that he is not happy about Macbeth's association with the witches.

1–5. As usual in the daylight of the Elizabethan theatre, it is necessary for Shakespeare to convey the time of day with words.

4. *There's husbandry in heaven:* 'They are being thrifty up in heaven' (they have put their candles – stars – out).

5. *that:* Having given Fleance his sword Banquo probably hands him his shield or cloak or dagger. Then, when Macbeth enters (line 9) his first instinct is to ask for his sword back, quickly.

6. *A heavy summons:* i.e. to sleep.

13. *unusual pleasure:* Probably because he is so appreciative of Macbeth's recent services and so confident of his thane.

14. *largess:* generous gifts.

offices: servants' quarters.

15. *withal:* with.

16–17. *shut up In measureless content:* Duncan's day has ended in unlimited happiness.

17–19. *Being unprepar'd . . . have wrought:* Because we were not prepared, our wish to provide the king with generous hospitality could not be fulfilled.

66

ACT TWO

Inverness. Court of Macbeth's castle

    Enter BANQUO, *and* FLEANCE *with a torch before him*

Banquo
  How goes the night, boy?
Fleance
  The moon is down; I have not heard the clock.
Banquo
  And she goes down at twelve.
Fleance   I tak't, 'tis later, sir.
Banquo
  Hold, take my sword. There's husbandry in heaven;
  Their candles are all out. Take thee that too.   5
  A heavy summons lies like lead upon me,
  And yet I would not sleep. Merciful powers
  Restrain in me the cursed thoughts that nature
  Gives way to in repose!

    Enter MACBETH *and a* SERVANT *with a torch*

                  Give me my sword.
  Who's there?   10
Macbeth
  A friend.
Banquo
  What, sir, not yet at rest? The king's a-bed.
  He hath been in unusual pleasure, and
  Sent forth great largess to your offices.
  This diamond he greets your wife withal,   15
  By the name of most kind hostess; and shut up
  In measureless content.
Macbeth   Being unprepar'd,

22–4. *Yet, when . . . the time:* When we can find a convenient time, let us talk about the witches – if you are willing to do so.

25–6. These words of Macbeth's are veiled and deliberately ambiguous. They could mean 'If you will follow my advice at the appropriate time' or 'If you will become a member of my party (*consent*) when it comes into existence'. If Banquo had ambitious ideas he could read enough into such words to ally himself with Macbeth; instead he makes it perfectly clear that he has no intention of getting mixed up in anything illicit. In the process he inevitably reveals to Macbeth that he has certain suspicions of him.

27. *augment:* increase.

28. *bosom franchis'd and allegiance clear:* my conscience free from guilt and my allegiance innocent.

29. *I shall be counsell'd:* I will accept your advice.

33–49. In the first part of this soliloquy Macbeth is revealed even more deeply than usual in such speeches, for the illusion of the bloody dagger shows us what we would now call his subconscious mind. Like Lady Macbeth he is denying his own true nature in preparing to commit the murder, and one of the penalties is a *heat-oppressed brain*.

36–7. *sensible To feeling as to sight?* touchable as well as visible?

39. *heat-oppressed:* feverish.

40. *palpable:* touchable.

42. The dagger must be moving towards Duncan's bedroom, as though it is encouraging Macbeth to go and do the deed.

Our will became the servant to defect;
Which else should free have wrought.
Banquo   All's well.
I dreamt last night of the three Weird Sisters.   20
To you they have show'd some truth.
Macbeth   I think not of them;
Yet, when we can entreat an hour to serve,
We would spend it in some words upon that business,
If you would grant the time.
Banquo   At your kind'st leisure.
Macbeth
If you shall cleave to my consent, when 'tis,   25
It shall make honour for you.
Banquo   So I lose none
In seeking to augment it, but still keep
My bosom franchis'd and allegiance clear,
I shall be counsell'd.
Macbeth   Good repose the while!
Banquo
Thanks, sir; the like to you!   30

Exeunt BANQUO *and* FLEANCE

Macbeth
Go bid thy mistress, when my drink is ready,
She strike upon the bell. Get thee to bed.

Exit SERVANT

Is this a dagger which I see before me,
The handle toward my hand? Come, let me clutch thee.
I have thee not, and yet I see thee still.   35
Art thou not, fatal vision, sensible
To feeling as to sight? or art thou but
A dagger of the mind, a false creation,
Proceeding from the heat-oppressed brain?
I see thee yet, in form as palpable   40
As this which now I draw.
Thou marshall'st me the way that I was going;

44–5. *Mine eyes . . . the rest:* Either my eyes are deceived (my other senses tell me there is no dagger) or else they are worth all my other senses put together (what I see really is a dagger).

46. *dudgeon:* handle.

gouts: drops.

48. *the bloody business:* the murder plan playing on his imagination.

49. *the one half-world:* the darkened northern hemisphere.

49–61. More clearly than ever Macbeth knows that, by murdering Duncan, he is associating himself with everything in and beyond the world that is wicked.

51. *curtain'd sleep:* sleep behind closed eyelids, or behind the curtains of a four-poster bed.

52. *Pale Hecate's offerings:* the ceremonies associated with Hecate, the goddess of witchcraft, who appears later in the play (Act III, Scene v and Act IV, Scene i).

52–6. *and wither'd murder . . . ghost:* Murder, personified as an aged, perhaps skeleton-like man, is awakened by the howl of a wolf, which keeps the time for him, and he moves stealthily, ghost-like (or in the same way that Tarquin went to rape Lucretia), to do his killing. Tarquin was an infamous King of Ancient Rome who raped the very virtuous Lucretia.

56–60. Macbeth is now in such a strange state of detachment that he asks the *firm-set earth* to prevent the stones he is walking on from announcing his presence, not because this will give him away, but because a horrible silence is appropriate to the deed.

58. *prate:* talk.

60. *threat:* threaten.

61. He is telling himself to stop talking and get on with it.

62. The sound of the bell prefaces the murder; the sound of knocking on the gate follows it.

63. *knell:* a funeral bell.

SCENE II

1–2. In Act I, Scene vii, lines 64–73, Lady Macbeth had said she intended to make the servants drunk and incapable of doing their duty properly in guarding the king. She now reveals that she, too, has been drinking, but in her case the effect has been to give her an artificial courage. Is this perhaps another sign that she is not quite as tough as she seems?

2. *quench'd:* put them out (like extinguished candles); in contrast, Lady Macbeth has been 'set alight' by the drink.

Hark! in spite of everything she is still capable of being frightened, in this case by an owl's cry.

3. The cry of an owl was thought to indicate that someone was about to die. This superstition still exists in some parts of England.

3–4. *the fatal bellman . . . good-night:* the night before a man was to be executed an official used to ring a bell outside the door of his cell.

stern'st good-night: the most serious, the final farewell, when a man is about to die.

4. *He is about it:* Macbeth is now murdering the king.

And such an instrument I was to use.
Mine eyes are made the fools o' th' other senses,
Or else worth all the rest. I see thee still;   45
And on thy blade and dudgeon gouts of blood,
Which was not so before. There's no such thing:
It is the bloody business which informs
Thus to mine eyes. Now o'er the one half-world
Nature seems dead, and wicked dreams abuse   50
The curtain'd sleep; now witchcraft celebrates
Pale Hecate's offerings; and wither'd murder,
Alarum'd by his sentinel, the wolf,
Whose howl's his watch, thus with his stealthy pace,
With Tarquin's ravishing strides, towards his design   55
Moves like a ghost. Thou sure and firm-set earth,
Hear not my steps which way they walk, for fear
Thy very stones prate of my whereabout
And take the present horror from the time,
Which now suits with it. Whiles I threat, he lives;   60
Words to the heat of deeds too cold breath gives.

A bell rings

I go, and it is done; the bell invites me.
Hear it not, Duncan, for it is a knell
That summons thee to heaven or to hell.

Exit

SCENE II—*Inverness.   Macbeth's castle*

Enter LADY MACBETH

Lady Macbeth
   That which hath made them drunk hath made me bold;
   What hath quench'd them hath given me fire. Hark!
      Peace!
   It was the owl that shriek'd, the fatal bellman,
   Which gives the stern'st good-night. He is about it.

5. Lady Macbeth must have left the doors open herself when she had finished dealing with the grooms.

surfeited: having had too much of something, in this case strong drink. The word *groom* was applied to any low-grade servant. These grooms are attendants on the king who act as bodyguards.

6. *mock their charge with snores:* they show how hopelessly they have failed by snoring while on duty.

drugg'd their possets: a posset was a nightcap containing milk, egg and some alcoholic drink, with other ingredients. Lady Macbeth had made quite sure that the men would be put out of action by adding a drug to the drink.

7. *nature:* life. Life and death are here thought of as two persons each of whom argues that the grooms belong to him.

8. Like his wife, Macbeth is startled by a sound. The effect of his frightened shout is all the greater because it comes from off-stage.

10–11. *Th' attempt ... Confounds us:* if, as I fear, he has tried to kill the king but failed, we shall be ruined.

11. *I laid their daggers ready:* Lady Macbeth's preparations have not been consistent. First she intended to kill Duncan herself (Act I, Scene v, line 52); then it seems that she thought of the two of them doing it together (Act I, Scene vii, line 70); in fact she has taken the grooms' daggers out of their scabbards and left them ready for Macbeth to do the stabbing. In his absent-minded horror Macbeth comes in with these daggers. How do you think he is carrying them?

13. *My husband!* what emotions do you think are packed into these words? Surprise? Admiration? Any others?

15. Both owls and crickets were thought to foretell death.

16–20. The jerky conversation obviously adds to the tension in the audience and also shows how jumpy Macbeth and his wife are.

19. Why does Lady Macbeth mention only Donalbain, when Malcolm too seems to be sleeping in the *second chamber* (next room)?

20. *sorry:* wretched, miserable.

22. These two men are almost certainly the king's sons and not the grooms.

The doors are open; and the surfeited grooms   5
Do mock their charge with snores. I have drugg'd their
    possets,
That death and nature do contend about them,
Whether they live or die.
Macbeth [*within*]   Who's there! What, ho!
Lady Macbeth
Alack! I am afraid they have awak'd,
And 'tis not done. Th' attempt, and not the deed,   10
Confounds us. Hark! I laid their daggers ready;
He could not miss 'em. Had he not resembled
My father as he slept, I had done't.

                    Enter MACBETH

                              My husband!

Macbeth
I have done the deed. Didst thou not hear a noise?
Lady Macbeth
I heard the owl scream and the crickets cry.   15
Did not you speak?
Macbeth   When?
Lady Macbeth   Now.
Macbeth   As I descended?
Lady Macbeth
Ay.
Macbeth
Hark!
Who lies i' th' second chamber?
Lady Macbeth   Donalbain.
Macbeth [*looking on his hands*]
This is a sorry sight.   20
Lady Macbeth
A foolish thought to say a sorry sight.
Macbeth
There's one did laugh in's sleep, and one cried 'Murder!'
That they did wake each other. I stood and heard them;
But they did say their prayers, and address'd them
Again to sleep.

25. *There are two lodg'd together:* Lady Macbeth is pointing out that, as the two princes are sharing a room, the disturbance may be confined to them.

27. *hangman's hands:* the word *hangman* was used for an executioner, whatever method he used; but since he usually 'drew' and 'quartered' the body (disembowelled it and cut it into pieces) even when the man had been hanged, a hangman's hands would often have been covered with blood. As the executions after the Gunpowder Plot had taken place not long before Shakespeare wrote the play, the picture of a hangman with his hands dripping blood would have been horribly vivid and familiar to his audience.

28. *List'ning their fear:* We should say 'listening to'.

35–9. In this speech Macbeth expresses his horror at the fact that he has killed a man in the helpless innocence of sleep; in his imagination he condemns himself to a fitting punishment – never to sleep again. Several poets of the time had written poems on sleep as Nature's gentle restorer and refuge from suffering, so these lines would have had a special irony for some of the onlookers.

37. *knits up the ravell'd sleave:* probably *sleave* means a piece of coarse silk; it has become (as we say) unravelled, but can be restored by knitting or stitching. In modern terms, sleep helps to soothe frayed nerves.

38. *sore labour's bath:* a good hot bath after a hard day's work, as it were.

39–40. *great nature's second course, Chief nourisher in life's feast:* a pudding or sweet used to be the first course at dinner; the main meat dish came after it.

44. Lady Macbeth, always more practical than her husband, is puzzled to know who could have been making the frightening comments about sleep.

45–6. She shows a familiar reaction to evidence of mental instability; 'Pull yourself together and don't be silly (brainsick)!'

46. *Go, get some water* . . . an apparently sensible, realistic way of dealing with the situation, but it proves altogether inadequate for herself as well as for her husband. (See Act V, Scene i, line 40: *What, will these hands ne'er be clean?*)

47. *witness:* evidence.

52. *Infirm of purpose!* Lady Macbeth's most effective way of bullying her husband is to comment scornfully on his weak will.

Lady Macbeth   There are two lodg'd together.   25
Macbeth

One cried 'God bless us,' and 'Amen' the other,
As they had seen me with these hangman's hands.
List'ning their fear, I could not say 'Amen'
When they did say 'God bless us!'
Lady Macbeth

Consider it not so deeply.   30
Macbeth

But wherefore could not I pronounce 'Amen'?
I had most need of blessing, and 'Amen'
Stuck in my throat.
Lady Macbeth   These deeds must not be thought
After these ways: so, it will make us mad.
Macbeth

Methought I heard a voice cry 'Sleep no more;   35
Macbeth does murder sleep'—the innocent sleep,
Sleep that knits up the ravell'd sleave of care,
The death of each day's life, sore labour's bath,
Balm of hurt minds, great nature's second course,
Chief nourisher in life's feast.
Lady Macbeth   What do you mean?   40
Macbeth

Still it cried 'Sleep no more' to all the house;
'Glamis hath murder'd sleep; and therefore Cawdor
Shall sleep no more—Macbeth shall sleep no more'.
Lady Macbeth

Who was it that thus cried? Why, worthy Thane,
You do unbend your noble strength to think   45
So brainsickly of things. Go get some water
And wash this filthy witness from your hand.
Why did you bring these daggers from the place?
They must lie there. Go carry them, and smear
The sleepy grooms with blood.
Macbeth   I'll go no more: 50
I am afraid to think what I have done;
Look on't again I dare not.

53–5. *The sleeping . . . devil:* she sounds strong and confident now, in contrast with Macbeth, yet earlier in this very scene (lines 12–13) she saw Duncan with *the eye of childhood* herself, and could not kill him.

55. *A painted devil:* a mere picture of a devil.

56–7. *gild the faces:* make them golden. Her use of the word *guilt* is a pun on 'gilt', a layer of gold. Do you find such punning out of place at such a terrible moment? For us today puns have come down in the world but for the Elizabethans they often conveyed tension and irony, not just rather obvious humour.

57. *Whence is that knocking?* Macbeth takes the knocking at first to be a supernatural thing. In the next scene it becomes known that Macduff and Lennox have been knocking at the castle gate in order to come in and rouse the king.

59. Macbeth is becoming so obsessed with the sight of his own bloody hands that they almost blind him.

60. Neptune was the Roman god of the sea.

61–3. Again Macbeth's imagination runs away with him. He believes that if he tries to wash his hands in the sea the blood will make the whole ocean red, there is so much of it smeared on them.

62. *multitudinous:* vast.

incarnadine: turn red (literally flesh-coloured). After putting this wildly imaginative idea in long words derived from Latin, Shakespeare almost repeats it in short Anglo-Saxon words.

63. *one red:* entirely red; red all over.

65. *a heart so white:* accusations of cowardice are another of Lady Macbeth's weapons against her husband.

67. She sounds confident but she too is later obsessed with the impossibility of washing the blood away (Act V, Scene i).

70. They have not changed into their night-clothes so far. She reminds him to do so, otherwise those who are knocking will think it strange that they are up and about, fully-clothed, in the middle of the night.

73. Macbeth knows that he cannot face fully the deed he has done, and take responsibility for it.

Lady Macbeth   Infirm of purpose!
  Give me the daggers. The sleeping and the dead
  Are but as pictures; 'tis the eye of childhood
  That fears a painted devil. If he do bleed,   55
  I'll gild the faces of the grooms withal,
  For it must seem their guilt.

                    Exit.   Knocking within

Macbeth   Whence is that knocking?
  How is't with me, when every noise appals me?
  What hands are here? Ha! they pluck out mine eyes.
  Will all great Neptune's ocean wash this blood   60
  Clean from my hand? No; this my hand will rather
  The multitudinous seas incarnadine,
  Making the green one red.

                    Re-enter LADY MACBETH

Lady Macbeth
  My hands are of your colour; but I shame
  To wear a heart so white. [*Knock*] I hear a knocking   65
  At the south entry; retire we to our chamber.
  A little water clears us of this deed.
  How easy is it then! Your constancy
  Hath left you unattended. [*Knock*] Hark! more knocking.
  Get on your nightgown, lest occasion call us   70
  And show us to be watchers. Be not lost
  So poorly in your thoughts.
Macbeth
  To know my deed, 'twere best not know myself. [*Knock*]
  Wake Duncan with thy knocking! I would thou couldst!

                    Exeunt

MACBETH

SCENE III

This drunken Porter has always been a controversial figure. Even such an important Shakespearian critic as Coleridge felt sure that Shakespeare couldn't have written the first part of this scene. But others have regarded the first 42 lines as very important, for the following reasons: the audience require some relief after the tension of the previous scene; there is a compelling irony about the fact that the Porter compares himself with the *porter of hell gate*, and this is almost what he is – certainly Macbeth has just acted and spoken as though he is in hell; finally, the insistent knocking to which the Porter is slowly responding is about to bring Macduff and Lennox on the scene, outsiders who become representatives of ordinary human decency.

2. The word *old* was often used in the sense of much, a lot of.

4. *Beelzebub:* Satan's lieutenant – but the name is often used of the Devil himself.

4–5. *Here's a farmer . . . plenty:* The Porter imagines himself to be a kind of guide showing us round Hell. The first of the damned he sees is a farmer who has committed suicide because the good harvest will put the price of corn down.

5–6. *Come in time . . . sweat for't:* Come early, then you can enjoy the bonfire of Hell and sweat freely, so you'll need cloths to wipe yourself.

7. *i' th' other devil's name?* It sounds as though the Porter cannot remember the name of any other devil.

8. *equivocator:* Probably a Jesuit priest, because the Jesuits were then believed to use words deceptively (to equivocate) in their defence against charges of treason. A Jesuit called Garnet (or sometimes Farmer) was tried in 1606 in connection with the Gunpowder Plot (to blow up the Houses of Parliament). Probably Shakespeare had him in mind.

9. *the scales:* Justice, personified as a woman, held scales in which to balance the evidence. If Shakespeare is here thinking of Father Garnet this is a comment on the way he equivocated at his trial.

10–11. *could not equivocate to heaven:* Garnet was hanged and that ended all his equivocation.

12–13. *an English tailor . . . French hose:* Tailors had a reputation for making clothes their customers ordered with the minimum of material and keeping the rest themselves. French hose had been very full and loose, and this gave the thieving tailors plenty of scope. But the French fashion had recently changed and tight hose made it obvious when they got up to their cloth-stealing tricks.

14. *roast your goose:* A goose was a tailor's smoothing-iron, but the phrase probably also meant something like 'kill the goose that laid the golden eggs', i.e. the tailor has tried his trick once too often and will profit no more from stealing customers' material.

16. *devil-porter it:* act the part of porter of Hell.

18. *the primrose way . . . bonfire:* the pleasant, easy path to Hell.

19–20. *remember the porter:* He is suggesting that they should tip him (even though he has taken so long to open the gate).

23. *carousing:* drinking riotously.

second cock: This was a way of saying 'three o'clock in the morning'.

SCENE III—*Inverness.   Macbeth's castle*

Knocking within.   Enter a PORTER

Porter

Here's a knocking indeed! If a man were porter of
hell-gate, he should have old turning the key. [*Knock*]
Knock, knock, knock! Who's there, i' th' name of
Beelzebub? Here's a farmer that hang'd himself on
th' expectation of plenty. Come in time; have napkins   5
enow about you; here you'll sweat for't. [*Knock*]
Knock, knock! Who's there, i' th' other devil's name?
Faith, here's an equivocator, that could swear in both
the scales against either scale; who committed treason
enough for God's sake, yet could not equivocate to   10
heaven. O, come in, equivocator. [*Knock*] Knock,
knock! Who's there? Faith, here's an English tailor
come hither for stealing out of a French hose. Come
in, tailor, here you may roast your goose. [*Knock*]
Knock, knock; never at quiet! What are you? But this   15
place is too cold for hell. I'll devil-porter it no further.
I had thought to have let in some of all professions
that go the primrose way to th' everlasting bonfire.
[*Knock*] Anon, anon! [*Opens the gate*] I pray you remember the porter.   20

Enter MACDUFF *and* LENNOX

Macduff

Was it so late, friend, ere you went to bed, that you
do lie so late?

Porter

Faith, sir, we were carousing till the second cock;

23–40. In this conversation the Porter plays the part of a typical Elizabethan stage working-man, obscenely witty and relishing playing with words, while Macduff is the condescending upper-class listener, willing to go along with the 'prole' for a while.

26. *nose-painting:* getting yourself a red nose.
Lechery: lust.

29. *equivocator:* deceiver.

33. *equivocates him in a sleep:* sends him to sleep and gives him lustful dreams (but no satisfaction for his lust).
33–4 & 35. *giving him the lie . . . gave thee the lie:* These could mean 'to lay out', as in wrestling or boxing.

36–9. The Porter gleefully plays with the wrestling metaphor and the idea of relieving himself.
requited him: paid him back.
made a shift: managed.

42. *Good morrow:* Good morning.

44. *timely:* early.
45. *slipp'd the hour:* missed my appointment.

46–7. 'I know this is a duty that you take pleasure in, but still it is an inconvenience'. Macbeth replies in the elaborately polite style that he seems to affect at times of strain.

and drink, sir, is a great provoker of three things.

Macduff

What three things does drink especially provoke?   25

Porter

Marry, sir, nose-painting, sleep, and urine. Lechery,
sir, it provokes and unprovokes; it provokes the
desire, but it takes away the performance. Therefore
much drink may be said to be an equivocator with
lechery: it makes him, and it mars him; it sets him on,   30
and it takes him off; it persuades him, and disheartens
him; makes him stand to, and not stand to; in conclu-
sion, equivocates him in a sleep, and, giving him the
lie, leaves him.

Macduff

I believe drink gave thee the lie last night.   35

Porter

That it did, sir, i' the very throat on me; but I requited
him for his lie; and, I think, being too strong for him,
though he took up my legs sometime, yet I made a
shift to cast him.

Macduff

Is thy master stirring?   40

Enter MACBETH

Our knocking has awak'd him; here he comes.

Lennox

Good morrow, noble sir!

Macbeth   Good morrow, both!

Macduff

Is the King stirring, worthy Thane?

Macbeth   Not yet.

Macduff

He did command me to call timely on him;
I have almost slipp'd the hour.

Macbeth   I'll bring you to him.   45

Macduff

I know this is a joyful trouble to you;

48. *physics pain:* acts as medicine to the pain (in this case the inconvenience) and removes it.

50. *limited:* appointed. Macduff has already explained that the King had instructed him to wake him early.

52. Do you think that Macbeth shows signs of hesitancy, or even guilt?

53–60. Lennox's description of the wild weather clearly suggests a supernatural origin for it. Very frequently in Shakespeare's work Nature reflects tragic or horrible events in human life. The speech also follows up the idea of the castle as the mouth of Hell. Macbeth has committed a highly unnatural act and this has wrenched Nature out of its usual channels.
57–8. *Of dire combustion . . . woeful time:* Terrible civil confusion developing out of this dreadful time.
58–9. *the obscure bird . . . night:* the owl [probably the Barn Owl, or Screech-owl] screamed right through the night. (See note on Act II, Scene ii, line 15).
59–60. *the earth Was feverous:* the earth trembled (in an earthquake) like a man in a fever.

61–2. There has never been such a night in my comparatively short life.

63–4. Strictly speaking Macduff has the two subjects the wrong way round; what he means is 'The imagination cannot conceive such a horror and the tongue cannot express it'.
65. *Confusion:* This was a very strong word, meaning something like utter chaos. This speech of Macduff's expresses the view of kingship as a potent symbol of all order, linked with the originator of order, God.

67. *The Lord's anointed temple:* Duncan, who like many kings, right down to the present day, was anointed with holy oil at his coronation.

But yet 'tis one.
Macbeth
The labour we delight in physics pain.
This is the door.
Macduff   I'll make so bold to call,
For 'tis my limited service.   *50*

Exit MACDUFF

Lennox
Goes the King hence to-day?
Macbeth
He does; he did appoint so.
Lennox
The night has been unruly. Where we lay,
Our chimneys were blown down; and, as they say,
Lamentings heard i' th' air, strange screams of death, *55*
And prophesying, with accents terrible,
Of dire combustion and confus'd events
New hatch'd to th' woeful time; the obscure bird
Clamour'd the livelong night. Some say the earth
Was feverous and did shake.
Macbeth   'Twas a rough night. *60*
Lennox
My young remembrance cannot parallel
A fellow to it.

Re-enter MACDUFF

Macduff
O horror, horror, horror! Tongue nor heart
Cannot conceive nor name thee.
Macbeth and Lennox   What's the matter?
Macduff
Confusion now hath made his masterpiece. *65*
Most sacrilegious murder hath broke ope
The Lord's anointed temple, and stole thence
The life o' th' building.
Macbeth   What is't you say—the life?

71. *a new Gorgon:* In the classical legend Medusa and her two sisters, all known as Gorgons, are represented as hideous women with snakes for hair who could turn to stone those who looked at them.

75. *downy sleep . . . counterfeit:* soft sleep, a gentle image of death.

77. *The great doom's image!* Macduff sees the murder of the King as comparable with the Day of Judgment at the end of the world.
78. *sprites:* ghosts (Macduff is continuing the idea of the Day of Judgment, when all the dead would rise from their graves to face (*countenance*) God.

81–2. That such a harsh trumpet calls those sleeping in the castle to a discussion (like opposing troops at a truce during war).

83–6. For the audience, there is a terrible irony in the idea of Lady Macbeth being too gentle and feminine to stand the awful news. *repetition:* report.

89. *What, in our house?* Several editors have thought that Lady Macbeth slipped up in saying these words, but they seem natural enough in the mouth of a supposedly horrified hostess.

Lennox
　Mean you his Majesty?
Macduff
　Approach the chamber, and destroy your sight　　　　70
　With a new Gorgon. Do not bid me speak;
　See, and then speak yourselves.

Exeunt MACBETH *and* LENNOX

　　　　　　　　　　Awake, awake!
　Ring the alarum bell. Murder and treason!
　Banquo and Donalbain! Malcolm! awake!
　Shake off this downy sleep, death's counterfeit,　　75
　And look on death itself. Up, up, and see
　The great doom's image! Malcolm! Banquo!
　As from your graves rise up and walk like sprites
　To countenance this horror! Ring the bell.

Bell rings. Enter LADY MACBETH

Lady Macbeth
　What's the business,　　　　　　　　　　80
　That such a hideous trumpet calls to parley
　The sleepers of the house? Speak, speak!
Macduff
　O gentle lady,
　'Tis not for you to hear what I can speak!
　The repetition in a woman's ear　　　　　　85
　Would murder as it fell.

Enter BANQUO

　　　　　　　　　O Banquo, Banquo,
　Our royal master's murder'd!
Lady Macbeth　　　　　　Woe, alas!
　What, in our house?
Banquo　　　　　　Too cruel anywhere.
　Dear Duff, I prithee contradict thyself,
　And say it is not so.　　　　　　　　90

91–6. Here is Macbeth's elaborate style again – as though he had prepared the speech beforehand. Supposing that Lady Macbeth pretends to faint soon afterwards, it is surely because she fears that her husband may overdo the wordy reaction and give them away.

91. *before this chance:* before what has happened.

93. There's nothing worth attention in the whole of human activity.

94. *toys:* triviality.

95–6. 'All the wine of life has been drawn from the cask and there is nothing but the dregs left', (*this vault:* presumably the earth). The whole of this speech of Macbeth's has a dreadful irony about it. He is striving to act the part of a loyal, sorrowing subject but in the process he is telling sombre truths about himself.

97. When Macbeth says the two young men are *amiss* he means they are ruined by their father's death.

98–9. *spring, head, fountain, source:* all describe the place at which a river or stream commences. Macbeth is using four words which mean the same thing.

101–5. The Macbeths must be pleased that Lennox puts the blame on the grooms, but later it appears that this explanation doesn't satisfy everyone.

badg'd: splotched (as though with red badges).

107. Macduff seems to express particular puzzlement about Macbeth's killing the grooms. Perhaps his doubts about Macbeth's character start here.

108–18. Questioned so directly Macbeth makes great verbal efforts to sound convincing, but produces a string of very forced metaphors, and possibly only succeeds in convincing his wife that she must do something to draw attention away from him.

110. *expedition:* rush.

111. *the pauser reason:* reason, which causes a person to delay before acting.

112. *silver skin . . . golden blood:* The picture is a vivid but very artificial one, and the language becomes more unnatural the longer he speaks.

Re-enter MACBETH, LENNOX, *with* ROSS

Macbeth
  Had I but died an hour before this chance,
  I had liv'd a blessed time; for, from this instant,
  There's nothing serious in mortality—
  All is but toys; renown and grace is dead;
  The wine of life is drawn, and the mere lees   *95*
  Is left this vault to brag of.

Enter MALCOLM *and* DONALBAIN

Donalbain
  What is amiss?
Macbeth   You are, and do not know't.
  The spring, the head, the fountain of your blood,
  Is stopp'd; the very source of it is stopp'd.
Macduff
  Your royal father's murder'd.
Malcolm   O, by whom?   *100*
Lennox
  Those of his chamber, as it seem'd, had done't.
  Their hands and faces were all badg'd with blood;
  So were their daggers, which unwip'd we found
  Upon their pillows. They star'd and were distracted;
  No man's life was to be trusted with them.   *105*
Macbeth
  O, yet I do repent me of my fury
  That I did kill them.
Macduff   Wherefore did you so?
Macbeth
  Who can be wise, amaz'd, temp'rate, and furious,
  Loyal and neutral, in a moment? No man.
  The expedition of my violent love   *110*
  Outrun the pauser reason. Here lay Duncan,
  His silver skin lac'd with his golden blood;
  And his gash'd stabs look'd like a breach in nature
  For ruin's wasteful entrance: there, the murderers,

116. *Unmannerly breech'd with gore:* This is the kind of language that, elsewhere, Shakespeare often makes fun of (see, for example, the First Player's speech in *Hamlet*, Act II, Scene ii). Macbeth is referring to the daggers as though they had trousers of blood on them right up to the hilts. This is one of a large number of images from clothing in the play (see the Theme Index at the end).

refrain: hold himself back (i.e. refrain from killing the grooms in righteous indignation).

118. There has been a great deal of discussion about Lady Macbeth's fainting-fit. Some think that she put it on in order to draw attention from her husband's over-acting; others regard it as the first sign that she is not as tough as she seems – the first stage in her decline into a pathetic, broken woman.

120–1. Why are we keeping quiet, since we (Duncan's sons) have the best reason to express grief?

122. *auger-hole:* an auger is the tool a carpenter uses for boring small holes. Donalbain is suggesting that their fate may be hidden nearby, ready to spring out and overwhelm them without warning (i.e. the murderer of their father may be prepared to kill them too). The expression also conveys the idea of the kind of hole made in a human body by a dagger.

124. People in the first shock of bereavement often find that they can't express their feelings freely by weeping. Donalbain is probably contrasting his own and his brother's reticence with Macbeth's noisy display.

125. *Upon the foot of motion:* ready to be expressed.

126. *naked frailties:* unclothed, weak bodies (all those present, apart from Macduff and Lennox, are still in their night-clothes). Is it possible also that Banquo is referring to emotions, proposing that they should all take a little time to recover their composure after the recent shocking events?

129. *scruples:* doubts.

130–2. Banquo makes it clear that he is committed to an honest, open way of life, and he loathes the deceit (*undivulg'd pretence*) and hate (*malice*) that have killed Duncan. (Some critics think that Banquo is already fearful that Malcolm may soon be killed also, and that the *undivulg'd pretence* is the intention to destroy him.)

133. *manly readiness:* either simply men's clothes or masculine qualities such as courage and determination.

135. *consort:* mix, associate.

136. *unfelt sorrow:* This does not imply that Malcolm is unaffected by his father's death. The brothers had agreed in lines 124–5 that they had not had time yet to be clear about their feelings and to express them.

office: duty.

Steep'd in the colours of their trade, their daggers　　*115*
Unmannerly breech'd with gore. Who could refrain,
That had a heart to love, and in that heart
Courage to make's love known?

Lady Macbeth　　　　　　　　　Help me hence, ho!
Macduff
　Look to the lady.
Malcolm [*aside to* DONALBAIN]
　Why do we hold our tongues that most may claim　　*120*
　This argument for ours?
Donalbain [*aside to* MALCOLM] What should be spoken
　Here, where our fate, hid in an auger-hole,
　May rush and seize us? Let's away.
　Our tears are not yet brew'd.
Malcolm [*aside to* DONALBAIN]　Nor our strong sorrow
　Upon the foot of motion.
Banquo　　　　　　　　　Look to the lady.　　*125*

　　　　LADY MACBETH *is carried out*

And when we have our naked frailties hid,
That suffer in exposure, let us meet,
And question this most bloody piece of work,
To know it further. Fears and scruples shake us.
In the great hand of God I stand, and thence　　*130*
Against the undivulg'd pretence I fight
Of treasonous malice.
Macduff　　　　　And so do I.
All　　　　　　　　　So all.
Macbeth
　Let's briefly put on manly readiness
　And meet i' th' hall together.
All　　　　　　　　Well contented.

　　　Exeunt all but MALCOLM *and* DONALBAIN

Malcolm
　What will you do? Let's not consort with them.　　*135*
　To show an unfelt sorrow is an office

137. It is pretty clear that *the false man* is Macbeth, and that Malcolm and Donalbain know who their enemy is.
easy: easily.
138–9. *our separated fortune . . . safer:* 'we'll be safer if we stay apart'. But why?
139–40. *Where we are . . . smiles:* 'Here in Scotland those who smile at us (i.e. Macbeth) are really our deadly enemies'. Does this suggest that Macbeth has gone out of his way in this scene to appear friendly? If you were producing the play and wanted to make this point, where would you instruct Macbeth to smile?
140–1. *the near in blood . . . bloody:* 'the man who threatens our lives is a relative' (Macbeth was Duncan's cousin).
141–2. *This murderous shaft . . . lighted:* An odd statement, because it has certainly *lighted* once already, on Duncan. It will light on others before long.
144. *dainty of leave-taking:* leave without ceremony.
145. *shift away:* slip away secretly (*shift* here has the meaning of planning or contriving to do something).
145–6. *There's warrant . . . left:* Malcolm is a little uneasy about running away, but justifies it on the grounds that their enemy is ruthless.
steals: 'goes stealthily away' as well as 'robs'.

SCENE IV

Shakespeare frequently gives us scenes in which strange and sinister events in Nature reflect human horrors and disasters. The disturbing things that Ross and the Old Man tell us about emphasize the unnaturalness of Macbeth's crime. Another purpose of the scene is to present Macduff as a decent man (he is referred to as *the good Macduff*) who strongly suspects Macbeth and is unwilling to give him any encouragement: Macduff refuses to go to Scone for Macbeth's coronation (line 36).

Stage Direction *Without:* outside. When Macduff enters he comes straight from the castle with the latest news.
1. *Threescore and ten:* the traditional life-span of a man is 70 years, so this Old Man, who must be nearly 80, looks back with particular authority; even he can recall nothing like the night that has just passed.
3–4. *this sore night . . . knowings:* this terrible night has made all previous experiences seem trivial.
5. *as:* as though.
6. *Threatens:* In Shakespeare's time this use of a singular verb with a plural subject was quite common.
his bloody stage: the stage on which man carries out his bloody deeds – that is, the earth. In the Elizabethan theatre the roof of the stage was called the 'heavens'.
7. *strangles the travelling lamp:* obscures the sun.
8–10. Ross suggests that the unnatural darkness may be accounted for by the triumph of evil, or by the unwillingness of the daylight to illuminate the dreadful deed.

Which the false man does easy. I'll to England.
Donalbain
   To Ireland I; our separated fortune
   Shall keep us both the safer. Where we are,
   There's daggers in men's smiles; the near in blood,   140
   The nearer bloody.
Malcolm   This murderous shaft that's shot
   Hath not yet lighted; and our safest way
   Is to avoid the aim. Therefore to horse;
   And let us not be dainty of leave-taking,
   But shift away. There's warrant in that theft   145
   Which steals itself, when there's no mercy left.

Exeunt

SCENE IV—*Inverness.   Without Macbeth's castle*

Enter ROSS *with an* OLD MAN

Old Man
   Threescore and ten I can remember well;
   Within the volume of which time I have seen
   Hours dreadful and things strange; but this sore night
   Hath trifled former knowings.
Ross   Ah, good father,
   Thou seest, the heavens, as troubled with man's act,   5
   Threatens his bloody stage. By th' clock 'tis day,
   And yet dark night strangles the travelling lamp.
   Is't night's predominance, or the day's shame,
   That darkness does the face of earth entomb,
   When living light should kiss it?
Old Man   'Tis unnatural,   10
   Even like the deed that's done. On Tuesday last,

12–13. *tow'ring* and *place:* terms from falconry. *tow'ring* means spiralling upwards to the *place* or 'pitch', which was the height from which a hawk 'stooped' or swooped down on to its prey. For an owl to attack and kill a falcon would have been unusual (though not perhaps quite unknown).
mousing: hunting mice.

15. *minions:* favourites – that is, the best of their kind.

16. *Turn'd wild in nature:* reverted to their wild state and were no longer domestic animals.
17. *as:* as if.
18. *eat:* the past tense, now spelt 'ate'.

23. Macduff gives the official line in his replies, but before the end of the scene it becomes evident that he has, privately, other ideas.

24. *pretend:* intend.
suborn'd: paid to do the deed.

27–9. Ross sounds a good deal more credulous than Macduff.
27. *'Gainst nature still:* Yet another unnatural event!
28. *Thriftless:* unprofitable.
ravin up: 'wolf', swallow greedily.
29. *Thine own life's means:* the source of their own life, i.e. their father.
like: likely.

30. New kings of Scotland were appointed by a form of election.
31. *Scone:* the ancient royal city; kings were crowned on the Stone of Destiny, which was supposed to be Jacob's pillow (see *Genesis* 28, verse 11). In 1296 Edward I of England took the stone to Westminster Abbey and, since then, all British sovereigns have been crowned on it.
32. *To be invested:* to go through the coronation ceremony.

A falcon, tow'ring in her pride of place,
Was by a mousing owl hawk'd at and kill'd.
Ross

And Duncan's horses—a thing most strange and
certain—
Beauteous and swift, the minions of their race,   15
Turn'd wild in nature, broke their stalls, flung out,
Contending 'gainst obedience, as they would make
War with mankind.
Old Man   'Tis said they eat each other.
Ross

They did so; to the amazement of mine eyes,
That look'd upon't.

Enter MACDUFF

                Here comes the good Macduff.   20
How goes the world, sir, now?
Macduff   Why, see you not?
Ross

Is't known who did this more than bloody deed?
Macduff

Those that Macbeth hath slain.
Ross   Alas, the day!
What good could they pretend?
Macduff   They were suborn'd.
Malcolm and Donalbain, the King's two sons,   25
Are stol'n away and fled; which puts upon them
Suspicion of the deed.
Ross   'Gainst nature still.
Thriftless ambition, that wilt ravin up
Thine own life's means! Then 'tis most like
The sovereignty will fall upon Macbeth.   30
Macduff

He is already nam'd, and gone to Scone
To be invested.
Ross   Where is Duncan's body?

33. *Colmekill:* The name means Colm's, or St Columba's, cell, on the island of Iona; this was where Scottish kings were buried.
34. *The sacred . . . predecessors:* the place where previous kings had been buried.

36. *Fife:* the home of Macduff, Thane of Fife.

37. *Well:* Macduff repeats, probably sarcastically, the *Well* of the unimaginative Ross. He doesn't sound at all hopeful that things will be *well done there.*

40. *benison:* blessing.
40–1. The Old Man's hopes are the first suggestion of a possible reversal of fortunes in the future. So far only those who would make bad of good have been successful.

Macduff
    Carried to Colmekill,
    The sacred storehouse of his predecessors
    And guardian of their bones.
Ross   Will you to Scone?   *35*
Macduff
    No, cousin, I'll to Fife.
Ross   Well, I will thither.
Macduff
    Well, may you see things well done there! Adieu,
    Lest our old robes sit easier than our new.
Ross
    Farewell, father.
Old Man
    God's benison go with you, and with those   *40*
    That would make good of bad, and friends of foes.

                        Exeunt

95

ACT THREE

SCENE I

Since we last saw Macbeth he has become quite smooth in his assurance. Banquo, on the other hand, has remained an honest and decent man – and is now almost certain that Macbeth became king by foul means. He, too, would like to have the witches' prophecies about him fulfilled, but has no intention of using Macbeth's methods to bring this about. Do you think he should have been more actively anti-Macbeth? Does Banquo strike you as someone with the right ideas, but without the determination to go through with them?

4. *It should . . . posterity:* Your descendants would not inherit the king-ship.

6. *them:* the witches.

7. *their speeches shine:* their words come true, in a brilliant way.

8. *verities:* truths.

9. *oracles:* An oracle, among the Greeks and Romans, was a person who acted as a mouthpiece of the gods. Banquo wonders whether the witches do perhaps tell the truth, and whether what they said about him may prove reliable.
10. *But, hush, no more:* Banquo dismisses his own ambitious thoughts.
Stage Direction *Sennet sounded:* a sennet was a series of notes on a trumpet, announcing an important arrival, such as that of a king.

11–13. Macbeth begins by deliberately flattering Banquo, and Lady Macbeth joins in with even more flowery language (there is an ominous echo of the Macbeths' invitation to Duncan).

13. *all-thing unbecoming:* totally unfitting.

14. *solemn:* formal (the word usually means this in Shakespeare).

15–18. The style of Banquo's response seems as artificial as the invitation. Do you blame him for this? (It is possible that, when he says *Let your Highness Command upon me*, he means 'If you, as King, order me, I haven't much alternative'. At least this may be what he implies.)

ACT THREE

Enter BANQUO

Banquo
  Thou hast it now—King, Cawdor, Glamis, all
  As the weird women promis'd; and I fear
  Thou play'dst most foully for't; yet it was said
  It should not stand in thy posterity;
  But that myself should be the root and father   5
  Of many kings. If there come truth from them—
  As upon thee, Macbeth, their speeches shine—
  Why, by the verities on thee made good,
  May they not be my oracles as well
  And set me up in hope? But, hush, no more.   10

    Sennet sounded. *Enter* MACBETH *as King*, LADY
    MACBETH *as Queen;* LENNOX, ROSS, LORDS, LADIES
           and ATTENDANTS

Macbeth
  Here's our chief guest.
Lady Macbeth   If he had been forgotten,
  It had been as a gap in our great feast,
  And all-thing unbecoming.
Macbeth
  To-night we hold a solemn supper, sir,
  And I'll request your presence.
Banquo   Let your Highness   15
  Command upon me; to the which my duties
  Are with a most indissoluble tie
  For ever knit.

19. The reason for this question, and the ones in lines 23 and 35, will soon become obvious. They are put privately to Banquo; the rest of the court should not hear them.

21. *which still . . . prosperous:* Which has always been well-considered and productive.
22. *but we'll take tomorrow:* I, the King, will have to hear your advice tomorrow instead.

25. *this:* now.
25-7. *Go not my horse . . . twain:* Unless my horse goes faster (than usual), it will have been dark for an hour by the time I get back.

29. *are bestow'd:* have settled.

31. *parricide:* killing a father.

32. The *strange invention* is that Macbeth was the murderer. Some time has gone by since the murder of Duncan, and Malcolm and Donalbain have no doubt been trying to gain support abroad by giving their version of what had happened.
33. *therewithal:* besides that.
33-4. *cause of state . . . jointly:* state affairs which will require our combined attention.
34. *Hie you:* Hurry.
36. *our time does call upon's:* we should be going.

40-3. You're all free to do as you wish until seven o'clock this evening; I will remain unattended until supper-time, so that human company will be all the pleasanter then.

43. *While:* Until.

44. *Attend those men our pleasure?* 'Are those men waiting for me?' (Macbeth must already have mentioned them to his servant.)

Macbeth
  Ride you this afternoon?
Banquo   Ay, my good lord.
Macbeth
  We should have else desir'd your good advice—   20
  Which still hath been both grave and prosperous—
  In this day's council; but we'll take to-morrow.
  Is't far you ride?
Banquo
  As far, my lord, as will fill up the time
  'Twixt this and supper. Go not my horse the better,   25
  I must become a borrower of the night
  For a dark hour or twain.
Macbeth   Fail not our feast.
Banquo
  My lord, I will not.
Macbeth
  We hear our bloody cousins are bestow'd
  In England and in Ireland, not confessing   30
  Their cruel parricide, filling their hearers
  With strange invention; but of that to-morrow,
  When therewithal we shall have cause of state
  Craving us jointly. Hie you to horse; adieu,
  Till you return at night. Goes Fleance with you?   35
Banquo
  Ay, my good lord; our time does call upon's.
Macbeth
  I wish your horses swift and sure of foot,
  And so I do commend you to their backs.
  Farewell.   [*Exit* BANQUO]
  Let every man be master of his time   40
  Till seven at night; to make society
  The sweeter welcome, we will keep ourself
  Till supper-time alone. While then, God be with you!

          Exeunt all but MACBETH *and a* SERVANT

  Sirrah, a word with you. Attend those men our pleasure?

45. *without:* outside.

46-7. *To be thus . . . safely thus:* Merely to be king is nothing; to be safely established on the throne is what's important.

47. *in:* of.

48. *Stick deep:* Are like thorns (or daggers) sticking in my flesh.

royalty of nature: Banquo was the ancestor of later Scottish (and English) kings, but the word *royalty* also suggests the kind of personal qualities that Macbeth himself lacks. One of the important things that become clear in this speech is that Macbeth envies Banquo's strong, manly qualities.

50. *to:* in addition to.

51-2. *He hath a wisdom . . . in safety:* We have seen this prudent side of Banquo earlier in the scene. Can you recall an occasion when he showed his *dauntless temper?*

53-5. *under him . . . by Caesar:* This refers to an old belief that one man's 'guardian angel' might be overcome by another's, resulting in the first man's destruction or obscurity. The Caesar referred to was Octavius Caesar who, although a younger and less brilliant man, defeated Mark Antony (see Shakespeare's *Antony and Cleopatra*).

55. *chid:* literally 'scolded', but 'spoke sternly to' might be a better version. If you look back to Act I, Scene iii, you will see that Banquo faced the witches boldly, almost contemptuously, before they made any prophecies. After they said that Macbeth would be king, Banquo demanded information about himself, but not in any subservient way.

59. *fruitless crown:* 'a crown that I would not be able to pass on'; *barren sceptre* in the next line is an exactly parallel phrase. *Crown* and *sceptre* were the two main symbols of kingship. It is worth remembering that many Englishmen had been deeply concerned about Queen Elizabeth not being married and not having an heir. Her father (Henry VIII) had been almost crazily keen to have a son to succeed him.

61. *with an unlineal hand:* 'by the hand of someone unrelated to me'. Macbeth hates the idea of someone else's son becoming king after him.

63. I have defiled my mind for the benefit of Banquo's descendants.

64. *gracious Duncan:* One of the terrible things about Macbeth's first crime is that he seems to have had a genuine admiration for Duncan, the man he murdered. (See Act I, Scene vii, lines 17-20.)

rancours: bitterness and hatred.

65-8. The *vessel* Macbeth has in mind may be the communion cup, because he goes on in religious terms.

eternal jewel: his immortal soul.

the common enemy of man: the Devil. What he seems to find intolerable is that he has thrown away his own hope of salvation in order to put Banquo's descendants (*seeds*) on the Scottish throne.

69-70. Roughly, Macbeth is saying 'Anything rather than that – I'd rather fight Fate itself to the bitter end'. The comparison is with a medieval tournament. The *list* was the enclosure in which such tournaments were held, to *champion* was to challenge, and 'à l'outrance' (*to th' utterance*) meant 'until one of the contestants died'.

71-140. After Macbeth has made sure that the servant cannot hear the following conversation he goes to great lengths to persuade the murderers (who are perhaps discarded army officers) to kill Banquo. It

First Murderer

It was, so please your Highness.

Macbeth   Well then, now

Have you consider'd of my speeches? Know

That it was he, in the times past, which held you   75

So under fortune; which you thought had been

Our innocent self. This I made good to you

In our last conference, pass'd in probation with you,

How you were borne in hand, how cross'd, the
    instruments,

Who wrought with them, and all things else that might   80

To half a soul and to a notion craz'd

Say 'Thus did Banquo.'

First Murderer   You made it known to us.

Macbeth

I did so; and went further, which is now

Our point of second meeting. Do you find

Your patience so predominant in your nature   85

That you can let this go? Are you so gospell'd,

To pray for this good man and for his issue,

Whose heavy hand hath bow'd you to the grave

And beggar'd yours for ever?

First Murderer   We are men, my liege.

Macbeth

Ay, in the catalogue ye go for men;   90

As hounds, and greyhounds, mongrels, spaniels, curs,

Shoughs, water-rugs, and demi-wolves, are clept

All by the name of dogs. The valued file

Distinguishes the swift, the slow, the subtle,

The house-keeper, the hunter, every one   95

According to the gift which bounteous nature

Hath in him clos'd; whereby he does receive

Particular addition, from the bill

That writes them all alike; and so of men.

Now, if you have a station in the file,   100

Not i' th' worst rank of manhood, say't;

And I will put that business in your bosoms

103

105–6. Macbeth declares that, as long as Banquo is alive, he cannot enjoy life like a healthy man. He is also suggesting that he is in constant danger from Banquo.

110. *tugg'd with fortune:* 'pushed around by fortune', as in a wrestling match.

112. *To mend it or be rid on't:* To improve my life or to put an end to it

114. *in such bloody distance:* in such mortal enmity.

115–16. *every minute . . . near'st of life:* 'every minute that he's alive I'm in desperate danger' (*thrusts Against my near'st of life* suggests a sword about to enter a vital part of the body).
117. *bare-fac'd power:* naked force.
118. *bid my will avouch it:* say that he is being destroyed simply because it happens to be my wish.
119. *For:* Because of.
120. *Whose loves . . . drop:* Whose respect and affection I don't want to lose.
120–1. *but wail . . . struck down:* but I must rather lament the death of the man I myself destroyed.
122. That I make such strong appeals for your assistance.

128. This is a puzzle. At the beginning of Act III, Scene iii, a mysterious Third Murderer joins the other two. Some people think he is *the perfect spy o' th' time.* But it's more likely that the phrase means 'the perfect observation (or estimation) of the time'.
130. *something from the palace:* a certain distance from the palace.
130–1. *always thought . . . a clearness:* in every circumstance, let it be understood that I must not be implicated.
131. *him:* Banquo.

THREE

Whose execution takes your enemy off,
Grapples you to the heart and love of us,
Who wear our health but sickly in his life,   *105*
Which in his death were perfect.

Second Murderer   I am one, my liege,
Whom the vile blows and buffets of the world
Hath so incens'd that I am reckless what
I do to spite the world.

First Murderer   And I another,
So weary with disasters, tugg'd with fortune,   *110*
That I would set my life on any chance,
To mend it or be rid on't.

Macbeth   Both of you
Know Banquo was your enemy.

Both Murderers   True, my lord.

Macbeth
So is he mine; and in such bloody distance
That every minute of his being thrusts   *115*
Against my near'st of life; and though I could
With bare-fac'd power sweep him from my sight,
And bid my will avouch it, yet I must not,
For certain friends that are both his and mine,
Whose loves I may not drop, but wail his fall   *120*
Who I myself struck down. And thence it is
That I to your assistance do make love,
Masking the business from the common eye
For sundry weighty reasons.

Second Murderer   We shall, my lord,
Perform what you command us.

First Murderer   Though our lives— *125*

Macbeth
Your spirits shine through you. Within this hour at most,
I will advise you where to plant yourselves,
Acquaint you with the perfect spy o' th' time,
The moment on't; for 't must be done to-night,
And something from the palace; always thought   *130*
That I require a clearness; and with him,

132. *no rubs nor botches:* 'no imperfections or errors' (they must make a thorough job of it).

134. *material:* important.

136. *Resolve yourselves apart:* Go away and make up your minds.

138. *I'll call upon you straight:* I shall require your services very soon.

SCENE II

This scene shows a striking change in the relationship between Macbeth and his wife. They are both disillusioned about the power and position they have gained at so great a cost; they both say that it's better to be dead than suffer the misery they are going through now. This is about all they agree on. Lady Macbeth is sinking into a kind of depressed fatalism, while Macbeth is planning more crimes in desperate schemes to assert himself and wipe out the possibility of Banquo's descendants inheriting the throne.

1. Lady Macbeth's first words suggest that she suspects her husband is plotting Banquo's death, but he has not told her about it.
3–4. *I would . . . a few words:* I should like to speak to him when he is free.

4–5. *Nought's had . . . without content:* We have done our utmost and achieved nothing; we've got what we wanted, but it has given us no happiness.
6–7. She seems almost to envy the dead Duncan and she says that the murder has not brought her any steady contentment.

9. With your own miserable fantasies as your only form of company.

To leave no rubs nor botches in the work,
Fleance his son, that keeps him company,
Whose absence is no less material to me
Than is his father's, must embrace the fate   *135*
Of that dark hour. Resolve yourselves apart;
I'll come to you anon.
Both Murderers   We are resolv'd, my lord.
Macbeth
   I'll call upon you straight; abide within.

                    Exeunt MURDERERS

It is concluded: Banquo, thy soul's flight
If it find heaven must find it out to-night.   *140*

                    Exit

SCENE II—*Forres.   The palace*

          Enter LADY MACBETH *and a* SERVANT

Lady Macbeth
   Is Banquo gone from court?
Servant
   Ay, madam, but returns again to-night.
Lady Macbeth
   Say to the King I would attend his leisure
   For a few words.
Servant   Madam, I will.

                    Exit

Lady Macbeth   Nought's had, all's spent,
   Where our desire is got without content.   5
   'Tis safer to be that which we destroy,
   Than by destruction dwell in doubtful joy.

                    Enter MACBETH

How now, my lord! Why do you keep alone,
Of sorriest fancies your companions making,

107

10–11. *those thoughts . . . they think on:* the fearful thoughts (of murder) should have stopped as soon as the murder was accomplished.

11–12. Lady Macbeth's double statement of fatalism. How do you account for her later collapse into *sorriest fancies* herself? (See Act V, Scenes i and ii.)

13. *scotch'd:* slashed (i.e. cut without killing).

14. *close:* join up again, be healed.

14–15. *our poor malice . . . former tooth:* our feeble ability to inflict harm is vulnerable to its regained power.

16. *But let the frame . . . suffer:* 'But let the whole universe collapse, and heaven and earth be destroyed . . .' (Shakespeare's tyrants often speak in this way, when desperate. Paranoia is the term we might apply today to such a state of mind).

19–22. *Better be . . . restless ecstasy:* Macbeth, without realizing it, repeats Lady Macbeth's thought in lines 6–7.

21. The image here is of a rack used to torture people.

22. *ecstasy:* frenzy, a state of mental turmoil.

23. *fitful fever:* a fever punctuated by times of great disturbance. (*fitful:* full of fits.)

24–6. *nor steel . . . touch him further:* assassination attempts with weapon or poison, rebellion at home, attack from abroad – none of these now has power to disturb Duncan.

27. *Gentle my lord:* It was quite common in Shakespeare's time to put the adjective in this position. The modern order is, of course, 'My gentle lord'.
sleek o'er your rugged looks: smooth away your worried looks.

30. Be particularly attentive to Banquo.

31. *Present him eminence:* Do him honour.

32. *Unsafe the while . . . what they are:* We are so unsafe at present that we must preserve our honour by flattering others, and mask our true feelings.

35. *You must leave this:* You must stop thinking like this.

38. Since Fleance is still very young, this certainly sounds like a hint to Macbeth that he can kill him and his father. Or perhaps she is probing to discover whether Macbeth is already committed to murdering them. (The line literally means 'The copyhold of Nature is not everlasting in them', i.e. as men they are mortal.)

Using those thoughts which should indeed have died   *10*
With them they think on? Things without all remedy
Should be without regard. What's done is done.
Macbeth
We have scotch'd the snake, not kill'd it;
She'll close, and be herself, whilst our poor malice
Remains in danger of her former tooth.   *15*
But let the frame of things disjoint, both the worlds
   suffer,
Ere we will eat our meal in fear and sleep
In the affliction of these terrible dreams
That shake us nightly. Better be with the dead,
Whom we, to gain our peace, have sent to peace,   *20*
Than on the torture of the mind to lie
In restless ecstasy. Duncan is in his grave;
After life's fitful fever he sleeps well;
Treason has done his worst; nor steel, nor poison,
Malice domestic, foreign levy, nothing,   *25*
Can touch him further.
Lady Macbeth   Come on.
Gentle my lord, sleek o'er your rugged looks;
Be bright and jovial among your guests to-night.
Macbeth
So shall I, love; and so, I pray, be you.
Let your remembrance apply to Banquo;   *30*
Present him eminence, both with eye and tongue—
Unsafe the while, that we
Must lave our honours in these flattering streams,
And make our faces vizards to our hearts,
Disguising what they are.
Lady Macbeth   You must leave this.   *35*
Macbeth
O, full of scorpions is my mind, dear wife!
Thou know'st that Banquo, and his Fleance, lives.
Lady Macbeth
But in them nature's copy's not eterne.

39. With her encouragement, Macbeth temporarily regains the feeling of partnership in hideous crime with his wife, and speaks of the planned murders in much the same way as he spoke of Duncan's as it approached – with revulsion and yet with a kind of relish.

40. *jocund:* joyful.

41. *cloister'd flight:* because bats often live in church buildings and can be seen flying in the cloisters in the evening.

black Hecate's summons: Hecate was the Greek goddess of witchcraft, and is therefore associated with darkness.

42. *shard-borne:* the expression could mean either (*a*) carried on wings like shards (pieces of pottery) or (*b*) born in cow-dung. The second is the more likely meaning.

43. *night's yawning peal:* the curfew-bell which announces the time for sleep.

45. *dearest chuck:* The familiar, affectionate expression could hardly be more incongruous at this point.

46–7. *Come ... day:* Macbeth is appealing to the night to hide his fearful crime from the light as falconers used to stitch together (*seel*) the eyes of a hawk when training it.

49–50. *that great bond ... pale:* what Shakespeare probably had in mind was the divine law against murder. Most moral laws seem to make Macbeth *pale* and fearful; he would like the commandments to be abolished for him so that he wouldn't feel afraid of breaking them.

50. *thickens:* grows dim.

50–1. *the crow ... rooky wood:* the crow (or rook) flies to its wood, which is already black with many birds.

53. The line conveys a chilling impression of supernaturally evil powers and of ferocious natural predators.

55. Macbeth seems to be getting his conscience under control, 'When one has done something evil to begin with, strength and security are gained by further evil'. The words seem to be said as some sort of reassurance: practice makes perfect, in evil as well as in good.

SCENE III

The appearance of an unexpected Third Murderer throws a little more light on Macbeth's present state of mind. He is so full of suspicion that he sets a thug to check up on thugs. Between them, the three are more than enough for Banquo, but Fleance manages to escape (as he must if Banquo's descendants are to inherit the Scottish throne).

2–4. We need not be suspicious (of this newcomer) since he has just given us instructions which are exactly like those Macbeth gave us himself.

Macbeth

There's comfort yet; they are assailable.
Then be thou jocund. Ere the bat hath flown   *40*
His cloister'd flight; ere to black Hecate's summons
The shard-borne beetle with his drowsy hums
Hath rung night's yawning peal, there shall be done
A deed of dreadful note.

Lady Macbeth   What's to be done?

Macbeth

Be innocent of the knowledge, dearest chuck,   *45*
Till thou applaud the deed. Come, seeling night,
Scarf up the tender eye of pitiful day,
And with thy bloody and invisible hand
Cancel and tear to pieces that great bond
Which keeps me pale. Light thickens, and the crow   *50*
Makes wing to th' rooky wood;
Good things of day begin to droop and drowse,
Whiles night's black agents to their preys do rouse.
Thou marvell'st at my words; but hold thee still:
Things bad begun make strong themselves by ill.   *55*
So, prithee go with me.

Exeunt

SCENE III—*Forres.   The approaches to the palace*

Enter three MURDERERS

First Murderer

But who did bid thee join with us?

Third Murderer   Macbeth.

Second Murderer

He needs not our mistrust, since he delivers
Our offices, and what we have to do,
To the direction just.

First Murderer   Then stand with us.
The west yet glimmers with some streaks of day;   *5*

6. *lated traveller:* one who is still journeying as night comes on.

7. *timely inn:* the inn he reaches just in time (before night is fully come).

8. *The subject of our watch:* Banquo.

10. *That . . . expectation:* That are expected (i.e. on the guest-list).

11. *go about:* take a roundabout route.

12–14. The whole murder-plan depends on the fact that people who arrive at the castle usually leave their horses with grooms and walk the last few hundred yards.

15. *Stand to't:* Be all ready to do the deed.

16. With macabre humour the First Murderer answers Banquo's comment on the weather with a remark that also refers to the rain of blows he and the others immediately deliver.

19. *Was't not the way?* Wasn't it the right thing to do?

20–1. Macbeth's emphasis on the need to kill Fleance as well as Banquo has clearly impressed itself on the murderers.

Now spurs the lated traveller apace
To gain the timely inn, and near approaches
The subject of our watch.

Third Murderer   Hark! I hear horses.

Banquo [*within*]
Give us a light there, ho!

Second Murderer   Then 'tis he; the rest
That are within the note of expectation   *10*
Already are i' th' court.

First Murderer   His horses go about.

Third Murderer
Almost a mile; but he does usually,
So all men do, from hence to th' palace gate
Make it their walk.

Enter BANQUO, *and* FLEANCE *with a torch*

Second Murderer   A light, a light!

Third Murderer   'Tis he.

First Murderer
Stand to 't.   *15*

Banquo
It will be rain to-night.

First Murderer   Let it come down.

Stabs BANQUO

Banquo
O, treachery! Fly, good Fleance, fly, fly, fly.
Thou mayst revenge. O slave!

Dies. FLEANCE *escapes*

Third Murderer
Who did strike out the light?

First Murderer   Was't not the way?

Third Murderer
There's but one down; the son is fled.

Second Murderer   We have lost   *20*
Best half of our affair.

113

SCENE IV

Macbeth has made the arrangements for his second crime with far less compunction than for the murder of Duncan but, during this scene, he certainly loses control of himself and shows extreme fear. Are these the same sort of misgivings as he showed over Duncan? By the end of the scene how do you consider he has regained control? Has Lady Macbeth's help been vital, or has Macbeth essentially relied on his own inner resources?

The scene can be quite simply staged, with thrones for Macbeth and his wife and a large table for the state banquet. Banquo's ghost is sometimes presented with scientific ingenuity, using mirrors, but nothing of this kind was attempted in Shakespeare's theatre. What method would you choose if you were directing a modern production?

1. *degrees:* respective rank, or seniority. This would determine where the guests sat at table.
2. From the beginning to the end of the banquet you are all heartily welcome.
4. *society:* the assembled guests.
6. *keeps her state:* stays seated on her throne.
in best time: at the right time.
7. *require her welcome:* request her to welcome you.

10. How do you imagine they show their thanks?

11. There seem to be equal numbers on both sides of the table. Where is it that Macbeth decides to sit (*i' th' midst*)?
12. *large:* generous (Macbeth encourages them to enjoy themselves freely, and to show it).
13. Macbeth sees one of the murderers at the door and moves over to speak to him. This is difficult to stage convincingly; how would you attempt it?

15. 'I prefer the blood to be outside you, not inside him'; another example of Macbeth's peculiarly grim humour.

First Murderer   Well, let's away,
And say how much is done.

Exeunt

SCENE IV—*Forres. The palace*

Banquet prepared. Enter MACBETH, LADY MACBETH,
ROSS, LENNOX, LORDS *and* ATTENDANTS

Macbeth
You know your own degrees, sit down.
At first and last the hearty welcome.
Lords
Thanks to your Majesty.
Macbeth
Our self will mingle with society
And play the humble host.   5
Our hostess keeps her state; but in best time
We will require her welcome.
Lady Macbeth
Pronounce it for me, sir, to all our friends;
For my heart speaks they are welcome.

Enter FIRST MURDERER *to the door*

Macbeth
See, they encounter thee with their hearts' thanks.   10
Both sides are even; here I'll sit i' th' midst.
Be large in mirth; anon we'll drink a measure
The table round.   [*Going to the door*]
There's blood upon thy face.
Murderer   'Tis Banquo's then.
Macbeth
'Tis better thee without than he within.   15
Is he despatch'd?
Murderer   My lord, his throat is cut;
That I did for him.

19. *the nonpareil:* the very best (unequalled).

21. *fit:* spasm of fear.
perfect: Macbeth seems to be continuing the health metaphor he used earlier (Act III, Scene i, lines 105–6).
22. *Whole:* firm.
founded: immovable.
23. As unlimited and free as the surrounding air.
24. *cabin'd, cribb'd, confin'd:* all these words mean 'shut up in a small space'. The alliteration produces emphasis.
25. *saucy:* impudent.

27. *trenched:* deeply cut.

28. The least of the cuts enough to kill a man.

29. *worm:* snake.

30. Will naturally, in time, develop the power to poison.

31–2. *to-morrow . . . again:* 'we'll hear each other again tomorrow', i.e. 'we'll meet and discuss the matter in detail'.

33. *give the cheer:* 'give encouragement' (as a host should) or possibly 'propose a toast'.
33–7. A banquet is like an ordinary meal that's paid for, unless the host frequently demonstrates his generous hospitality. If simple feeding is all that's wanted, that is best done at home. Away from home (*From thence*) the ritual of welcoming the guests is the best appetizer. A public occasion would be unimpressive without it.

37. *Sweet remembrancer!* Macbeth is thanking his wife for reminding him of his duties as host.

40. *our country's honour:* Macbeth's deliberately exaggerated way of referring to Banquo.

41. *grac'd:* gracious.

Macbeth   Thou art the best o' th' cut-throats;
Yet he's good that did the like for Fleance.
If thou didst it, thou art the nonpareil.
Murderer
Most royal sir—Fleance is 'scap'd.   20
Macbeth
Then comes my fit again. I had else been perfect,
Whole as the marble, founded as the rock,
As broad and general as the casing air,
But now I am cabin'd, cribb'd, confin'd, bound in
To saucy doubts and fears. But Banquo's safe?   25
Murderer
Ay, my good lord. Safe in a ditch he bides,
With twenty trenched gashes on his head,
The least a death to nature.
Macbeth   Thanks for that.
There the grown serpent lies; the worm that's fled
Hath nature that in time will venom breed,   30
No teeth for th' present. Get thee gone; to-morrow
We'll hear, ourselves, again.

                    Exit MURDERER

Lady Macbeth   My royal lord,
You do not give the cheer; the feast is sold
That is not often vouch'd, while 'tis a-making,
'Tis given with welcome. To feed were best at home: 35
From thence the sauce to meat is ceremony;
Meeting were bare without it.

        Enter the GHOST OF BANQUO *and sits in* MACBETH'S
                    place

Macbeth   Sweet remembrancer!
Now good digestion wait on appetite,
And health on both!
Lennox   May't please your Highness sit?
Macbeth
Here had we now our country's honour roof'd,   40
Were the grac'd person of our Banquo present;

42-3. Macbeth, with terrible insincerity, says that he hopes he can blame Banquo for bad manners, rather than feel anxious because ill fortune may have prevented him from attending.

43-4. *His absence . . . promise:* He shouldn't have said he was going to be present if he couldn't manage it.

46. Macbeth glances round the table and merely registers the fact that the seat he intended to sit in (the one *i' th' midst*) is now occupied. He doesn't at first see that Banquo's ghost is occupying it.

49. *Which of you have done this?* This is usually interpreted as 'Which of you killed Banquo?' Is it possible that Macbeth really suspects that someone has tried to trick him by staging the appearance of Banquo's ghost?

50-1. Macbeth disclaims responsibility because he didn't actually do the killing himself. Would it be true to say that it is always the messy side of murder that he dislikes and fears, rather than the moral issues involved?

52-5. Ross's remark about Macbeth's apparent illness gives Lady Macbeth an opportunity to make up a fairly convincing explanation on the spur of the moment.

upon a thought: in a moment.

56-7. If you take a great deal of notice of him you will only annoy him and enrage him even more.

58. *Are you a man?* Lady Macbeth's main method is the 'Pull yourself together' one, shaming him by her contemptuous comments.

60. *O proper stuff!* What you're saying is sheer rubbish!

61. *painting of your fear:* an imaginary representation brought about by fear, not real at all.

62. *air-drawn:* drawn in the air (and therefore insubstantial, unreal).

63. *flaws and starts:* wild fits. *flaw:* a sudden squall.

64. *Impostors to true fear:* again, she means 'not the real thing' – his frightened behaviour isn't based on anything that would properly inspire fear.

65-6. *A woman's . . . grandam:* An old wives' tale passed down from a previous generation.

66. *Shame itself!* You are the personification of shame.

Who may I rather challenge for unkindness
Than pity for mischance.

Ross   His absence, sir,
Lays blame upon his promise. Please 't your Highness
To grace us with your royal company.   45

Macbeth
The table's full.

Lennox   Here is a place reserv'd, sir.

Macbeth
Where?

Lennox   Here, my good lord.
What is't that moves your Highness?

Macbeth
Which of you have done this?

Lords   What, my good lord?

Macbeth
Thou canst not say I did it; never shake   50
Thy gory locks at me.

Ross
Gentlemen, rise; his Highness is not well.

Lady Macbeth
Sit, worthy friends. My lord is often thus,
And hath been from his youth. Pray you, keep seat.
The fit is momentary; upon a thought   55
He will again be well. If much you note him,
You shall offend him and extend his passion.
Feed, and regard him not.—Are you a man?

Macbeth
Ay, and a bold one that dare look on that
Which might appal the devil.

Lady Macbeth   O proper stuff!   60
This is the very painting of your fear;
This is the air-drawn dagger which you said
Led you to Duncan. O, these flaws and starts—
Impostors to true fear—would well become
A woman's story at a winter's fire,   65
Authoriz'd by her grandam. Shame itself!

119

69. *how say you?* there, what do you say to that? It's making gestures now!

70. *nod:* This often meant 'beckon' in Elizabethan English. Perhaps Banquo's ghost is, as it were, inviting Macbeth to join him in death.

71–3. *If charnel-houses . . . kites:* 'If men come back from the dead like this, the only way to dispose of a body completely will be to feed it to kites.' (Kites were common scavenger-birds in earlier times in England, as they still are in other parts of the world.)

charnel-houses: stores of bones dug up by grave-diggers.

maws: stomachs.

73. *unmann'd:* Lady Macbeth's standard reproach to her husband – 'You're not a real man any more, behaving in this crazy way'.

74. *Fie:* a contemptuous exclamation.

76–80. *Ere humane statute . . . an end:* 'Murders were committed in previous ages, before civilized laws cleansed society and made it more gentle, and they have been committed in more recent times, too – murders too horrible to describe – but in the past the murdered men died when their brains were knocked out, and that was the end of them . . .' (It seems ironical that Macbeth, a bloody criminal himself, should speak of *humane statute* purging the *gentle weal*, but these words reflect the deeply divided personality of the man; part of him really does respect the civilized virtues.)

81. *twenty mortal murders:* see lines 27–8. *twenty trenched gashes . . . The least a death to nature.*

crowns: heads.

82. *strange:* the word here, and in many other places in the play, means something like 'unnatural'. Macbeth nearly always acknowledges to himself the outrageousness of his deeds.

85. *muse at me:* be astonished at me.

88. *Then I'll sit down:* when the health has been drunk.

89–93. Banquo appears to Macbeth when he is being most hypocritical and least honest with himself. No-one else sees the ghost. Do you think, then, that it is a fantasy present only in Macbeth's mind? Should it be visible to the audience?

91. *we thirst:* we desire to drink.

92. *all to all:* let us all drink to each other.

Our duties, and the pledge: We offer our respects (to your Majesty) and drink the toast (you propose).

Why do you make such faces? When all's done,
You look but on a stool.
Macbeth   Prithee see there.
  Behold! look! lo! how say you?
  Why, what care I? If thou canst nod, speak, too.   *70*
  If charnel-houses and our graves must send
  Those that we bury back, our monuments
  Shall be the maws of kites. [*Exit* GHOST]
Lady Macbeth   What, quite unmann'd in folly?
Macbeth
  If I stand here, I saw him.
Lady Macbeth   Fie, for shame!
Macbeth
  Blood hath been shed ere now, i' th' olden time,   *75*
  Ere humane statute purg'd the gentle weal;
  Ay, and since too, murders have been perform'd
  Too terrible for the ear. The time has been
  That when the brains were out the man would die,
  And there an end; but now they rise again,   *80*
  With twenty mortal murders on their crowns,
  And push us from our stools. This is more strange
  Than such a murder is.
Lady Macbeth   My worthy lord,
  Your noble friends do lack you.
Macbeth   I do forget.
  Do not muse at me, my most worthy friends;   *85*
  I have a strange infirmity, which is nothing
  To those that know me. Come, love and health to all;
  Then I'll sit down. Give me some wine, fill full.

                      Enter GHOST

  I drink to the general joy o' th' whole table,
  And to our dear friend Banquo, whom we miss.   *90*
  Would he were here! To all, and him, we thirst,
  And all to all.
Lords   Our duties, and the pledge.

93. *Avaunt:* go away. At this moment all the lords are on their feet, ready to drink the toast. When Macbeth's *fit* comes again, no doubt they remain standing, aghast. Then, perhaps, they mutter among themselves as he continues to rave.

93–4. *Let the earth . . . cold:* you're a corpse; you should be in a grave.
95. *speculation:* light of intelligence.

97. *a thing of custom:* a quite normal happening.

99. Macbeth continues to address the ghost, oblivious of Lady Macbeth's attempt to calm the horrified lords. Nevertheless he is partly answering her charge of not being a man.
100. If you came in the form of a shaggy Russian bear.
101. *arm'd:* i.e. with a horn.
Hyrcan tiger: a tiger from Hyrcania, a region near the Caspian Sea.
102. *but that:* except the form of the dead Banquo.
104. Challenge me to fight with swords by ourselves in the desert.
105. *inhabit:* stay at home.
protest: declare.
106. *The baby of a girl:* a baby girl.
107. Lady Macbeth's insistence on the unreality of what he sees has had some effect on him. As soon as he asserts that the ghost is *Unreal*, it disappears.
being gone: now that it has gone.

109–10. You have destroyed the good humour and shattered a pleasant social occasion with an agitation that has astounded everyone.
111. *overcome:* pass over.

112–13. *You make me strange . . . owe:* 'You (i.e. all those present) make me doubtful of my own nature.' (Because he is deeply frightened, while they seem undisturbed by what he saw.)
I owe: that belongs to me.

116. *mine is blanch'd:* my natural colour (*ruby*) has been replaced by paleness.

118–20. *Question enrages him . . . :* It is clear that Lady Macbeth is not going to allow her husband to incriminate himself any further. She makes sure that they all leave without delay.
118. *At once, good night* Let me say good-night to all of you together.
119. Don't bother about seniority in leaving.

122

Macbeth

    Avaunt, and quit my sight. Let the earth hide thee.
    Thy bones are marrowless, thy blood is cold;
    Thou hast no speculation in those eyes   *95*
    Which thou dost glare with!

Lady Macbeth   Think of this, good peers,
    But as a thing of custom. 'Tis no other;
    Only it spoils the pleasure of the time.

Macbeth

    What man dare, I dare.
    Approach thou like the rugged Russian bear,   *100*
    The arm'd rhinoceros, or th' Hyrcan tiger;
    Take any shape but that, and my firm nerves
    Shall never tremble. Or be alive again,
    And dare me to the desert with thy sword;
    If trembling I inhabit, then protest me   *105*
    The baby of a girl. Hence, horrible shadow!
    Unreal mock'ry, hence!

Exit GHOST

                       Why, so; being gone,
    I am a man again. Pray you, sit still.

Lady Macbeth

    You have displac'd the mirth, broke the good meeting,
    With most admir'd disorder.

Macbeth   Can such things be, *110*
    And overcome us like a summer's cloud,
    Without our special wonder? You make me strange
    Even to the disposition that I owe,
    When now I think you can behold such sights
    And keep the natural ruby of your cheeks,   *115*
    When mine is blanch'd with fear.

Ross   What sights, my lord?

Lady Macbeth

    I pray you speak not; he grows worse and worse;
    Question enrages him. At once, good night.
    Stand not upon the order of your going,

121. As soon as she has ushered them all out she seems to be nervously exhausted. Her handling of this very difficult situation is in fact the last sign of her masterfulness. She now slips into the background while Macbeth becomes more and more committed to hideous destruction.

122. *It:* the murder of Banquo, or perhaps Banquo's ghost itself.

123. The stones are probably those which might cover the body of a murdered man.

trees: there are ancient stories of the gods and of ghosts speaking from trees.

124–6. *Augurs . . . man of blood:* Divinations (i.e. drawing conclusions from omens) and the understanding of connections between signs and events have revealed the most secret murderers, through the observation of birds' movements.

maggot-pies: magpies. *choughs:* crows or jackdaws. The augurs, or Roman priests, often made predictions from what they observed of birds in flight.

126. *What is the night ?* What time of night is it?

127. *Almost at odds with morning:* 'It's hard to say whether it's night or morning.' Professor Dover Wilson pointed out that this is a symbolic moment, the centre point of the play, when the darkness represented by Macbeth and all his works seems complete, but when the first signs of opposition (representing a new dawn) are about to appear (notice Macduff's defiance, referred to in the next line).

128. *How say'st thou . . . ?* What do you say to the fact that . . . ?

130. Lady Macbeth has asked him if he sent a messenger to Macduff; she wonders whether her husband received a direct rebuff. Macbeth replies that he heard of Macduff's attitude incidentally.

131–2. Macbeth employs spies in the houses of all his thanes. The picture of a cruel dictatorship maintained by fear in an atmosphere of suspicion becomes more complete.

I will tomorrow: I will send to Macduff tomorrow.

133. *betimes:* early, very soon.

134. *bent:* determined.

135–6. *For mine own good . . . give way:* Everything else must take second place to my welfare.

136–8. The image is, appropriately, of wading across a river of blood. He feels he is already wading so deeply that he may as well go on to the far side.

139–40. I have dark thoughts that will become deeds – the sort that have to be put into effect without being carefully considered first.

Strange: again, the word conveys a sense of unnaturalness.

141. By the end of the play they both conspicuously lack this *season* (preservative, spice). Macbeth has, as he says himself, *murder'd sleep* (Act II, Scene ii, line 42).

142–3. *My strange and self-abuse . . . hard use:* Those strange fantasies I thought I saw were merely the fears of a beginner lacking tough practice.

144. *We:* the royal 'we' rather than a plural covering himself and Lady Macbeth, since she has no share in his evil plans now.

But go at once.
Lennox   Good night; and better health *120*
 Attend his Majesty!
Lady Macbeth   A kind good night to all!
     Exeunt LORDS *and* ATTENDANTS
Macbeth
 It will have blood; they say blood will have blood.
 Stones have been known to move, and trees to speak;
 Augurs and understood relations have
 By maggot-pies and choughs and rooks brought
  forth   *125*
 The secret'st man of blood. What is the night?
Lady Macbeth
 Almost at odds with morning, which is which.
Macbeth
 How say'st thou that Macduff denies his person
 At our great bidding?
Lady Macbeth   Did you send to him, sir?
Macbeth
 I hear it by the way; but I will send— *130*
 There's not a one of them but in his house
 I keep a servant fee'd—I will to-morrow.
 And betimes I will to the Weird Sisters:
 More shall they speak; for now I am bent to know
 By the worst means the worst. For mine own good *135*
 All causes shall give way. I am in blood
 Stepp'd in so far that, should I wade no more,
 Returning were as tedious as go o'er.
 Strange things I have in head that will to hand,
 Which must be acted ere they may be scann'd. *140*
Lady Macbeth
 You lack the season of all natures, sleep.
Macbeth
 Come, we'll to sleep. My strange and self-abuse
 Is the initiate fear that wants hard use.
 We are yet but young in deed.
      Exeunt

SCENE V

It is unlikely that Shakespeare wrote this scene. The rhythm and style are quite different from those of the earlier scenes with the witches. Hecate's introduction into the play serves little purpose and the scene is usually cut in modern productions.

1. *Hecat:* (or Hecate) a goddess of witchcraft in Greek mythology.
angerly: angrily or, as we would say, 'angry'.
2. *beldams:* hags, hideous old women.

6. *charms:* magical powers.

7. Secret organizer of wickedness.

11. *wayward son:* unreliable pupil.

15. *pit of Acheron:* apparently the name of the witches' cave (*Acheron* was one of the rivers of Hell in classical legend).

20. *I am for th' air:* 'I am going up into the air' (like the traditional witch, popularly supposed to ride on a broomstick).
21. *Unto a dismal . . . end:* On a disastrous and ominous purpose.

23–9. It was believed that the moon shed a kind of dew on certain plants, and this liquid was highly prized for its magic qualities.
24. *vap'rous drop profound:* a drop of vapour with profound powers.

26. *sleights:* arts.

27. *artificial sprites:* spirits or apparitions conjured up by magic arts.

29. *confusion:* ruin.
30–1. *bear His hopes . . . fear:* he will become utterly careless of considerations such as commonsense, God's grace and natural fear, (swept away by the wild hopes the witches will give him.)

SCENE V—*A heath*

    Thunder.   *Enter the three* WITCHES, *meeting* HECATE

First Witch
  Why, how now, Hecat! You look angerly.
Hecate
  Have I not reason, beldams as you are,
  Saucy and overbold? How did you dare
  To trade and traffic with Macbeth
  In riddles and affairs of death;   *5*
  And I, the mistress of your charms,
  The close contriver of all harms,
  Was never call'd to bear my part,
  Or show the glory of our art?
  And, which is worse, all you have done   *10*
  Hath been but for a wayward son,
  Spiteful and wrathful; who, as others do,
  Loves for his own ends, not for you.
  But make amends now. Get you gone,
  And at the pit of Acheron   *15*
  Meet me i' the morning; thither he
  Will come to know his destiny.
  Your vessels and your spells provide,
  Your charms, and everything beside.
  I am for th' air; this night I'll spend   *20*
  Unto a dismal and a fatal end.
  Great business must be wrought ere noon.
  Upon the corner of the moon
  There hangs a vap'rous drop profound;
  I'll catch it ere it come to ground;   *25*
  And that, distill'd by magic sleights,
  Shall raise such artificial sprites
  As, by the strength of their illusion,
  Shall draw him on to his confusion.
  He shall spurn fate, scorn death, and bear   *30*
  His hopes 'bove wisdom, grace, and fear;

32. *security:* over-confidence.

Stage Direction This song occurs in a play called *The Witch* by Middleton, a contemporary of Shakespeare.

34–5. *little spirit:* Hecate's familiar. Probably the *foggy cloud*, in early productions, was a painted piece of wood lowered for Hecate to step on to; then she would be whisked up and out of sight.

SCENE VI

Since his last words in the Banquet Scene (*Good night; and better health Attend his Majesty!*) Lennox has obviously done some hard thinking. The deep irony of some of his remarks is very striking. Apart from the fact that some of the Scottish lords have now 'seen through' Macbeth, the scene provides the first suggestion of better things to come.

1–3. *My former speeches . . . borne:* The remarks I have recently made have only put into words what you were thinking already. You can work out things in greater detail for yourself. All I say is that things have been carried on in a very odd way.

3–4. *The gracious Duncan . . . Macbeth:* The suggestion is that Macbeth could afford to pity Duncan when he was dead.

5–7. Macbeth had put the blame for Duncan's death on Malcolm and Donalbain, because they had fled to England. Lennox sarcastically suggests that it's just as reasonable to say that Fleance killed his father, as he has fled, too.

8–10. Logically the sentence should begin 'who *can* want the thought . . . ?' (i.e. 'who can help thinking . . . ?'), and this is the main meaning. *monstrous:* unnatural.

10. *fact:* evil deed.

11. *straight:* immediately.

12. *pious:* loyal, patriotic.

delinquents: those who have failed in their duty.

13. *thralls:* can also mean slaves.

14–16. *Ay, and wisely . . . men deny't:* Without saying so, Lennox makes it clear that he thinks Macbeth was wise to kill the guards because they might have been able to convince the hearers of their innocence. Irony pervades the whole speech.

17. *He has borne all things well:* He has organized everything with remarkable skill.

18. *under his key:* locked up.

19. *an't:* if it.

20. Again very sarcastically, Lennox says that Macbeth would teach Malcolm, Donalbain and Fleance a lesson for killing their fathers.

And you all know security
Is mortals' chiefest enemy.
[*Music and a song within:* 'Come away, come away, etc.']
Hark! I am call'd; my little spirit, see,
Sits in a foggy cloud, and stays for me.   35

Exit

First Witch
   Come, let's make haste; she'll soon be back again.

Exeunt

SCENE VI—*Forres.   The palace*

Enter LENNOX *and another* LORD

Lennox
   My former speeches have but hit your thoughts,
   Which can interpret farther. Only I say
   Things have been strangely borne. The gracious Duncan
   Was pitied of Macbeth. Marry, he was dead.
   And the right-valiant Banquo walk'd too late;   5
   Whom, you may say, if't please you, Fleance kill'd,
   For Fleance fled. Men must not walk too late.
   Who cannot want the thought how monstrous
   It was for Malcolm and for Donalbain
   To kill their gracious father? Damned fact!   10
   How it did grieve Macbeth! Did he not straight,
   In pious rage, the two delinquents tear,
   That were the slaves of drink and thralls of sleep?
   Was not that nobly done? Ay, and wisely too;
   For 'twould have anger'd any heart alive   15
   To hear the men deny't. So that, I say,
   He has borne all things well; and I do think
   That had he Duncan's sons under his key—
   As, an't please heaven, he shall not—they should find
   What 'twere to kill a father; so should Fleance.   20

21. *broad:* outspoken, unrestrained.

23–4. *can you tell . . . himself?* do you know where he's staying?

24–5. *The son of Duncan . . . birth:* Malcolm, from whom the dictator Macbeth withholds his rightful inheritance (the throne of Scotland).

28–9. *That the malevolence . . . respect:* the fact that he's had such ill fortune doesn't reduce in any way the honour he receives (in the English court).

30. *the holy King:* Edward the Confessor's piety and the orderly, God-fearing atmosphere of England are stressed, and the contrast with Scotland, an unhappy land ruled by a monster, is pointed out, here and later.

upon his aid: on Malcolm's behalf.

31. *wake:* rouse. The Earl of Northumberland is later called 'Old Siward' and his *warlike* son 'Young Siward'.

32–3. *with Him above To ratify the work:* with God to strengthen their activities.

34–6. Have good food on our tables again, sleep well at night, hold banquets without the fear of bloody murder, pay sincere respect to a rightful king and receive from him honours freely earned . . .

38. *exasperate:* exasperated, irritated.

40–3. Macbeth sent for Macduff, as he told Lady Macbeth he would (Act III, Scene iv, line 130), but Macduff flatly rejected the summons (*Sir, not I!*); the surly (*cloudy*) messenger turned his back on Macduff and grunted, as if to say 'You'll live to regret burdening me with such an answer' (anyone who brought an unsatisfactory message to Macbeth was likely to suffer for it – see, for example, Act V, Scene v, lines 29–41).

43–5. *And that well might . . . provide:* That should be enough to warn Macduff to stay as far away as possible from Macbeth.

47. *His:* Macduff's.

48–9. *ou. ..uffering country . . . accurs'd!* our country, now suffering under a damned tyranny.

But peace! For from broad words, and 'cause he fail'd
His presence at the tyrant's feast, I hear,
Macduff lives in disgrace. Sir, can you tell
Where he bestows himself?

Lord   The son of Duncan,
  From whom this tyrant holds the due of birth,   *25*
  Lives in the English court, and is receiv'd
  Of the most pious Edward with such grace
  That the malevolence of fortune nothing
  Takes from his high respect; thither Macduff
  Is gone to pray the holy King upon his aid   *30*
  To wake Northumberland and warlike Siward,
  That by the help of these—with Him above
  To ratify the work—we may again
  Give to our tables meat, sleep to our nights,
  Free from our feasts and banquets bloody knives,   *35*
  Do faithful homage and receive free honours—
  All which we pine for now. And this report
  Hath so exasperate the King that he
  Prepares for some attempt of war.

Lennox   Sent he to Macduff?

Lord
  He did; and with an absolute 'Sir, not I!'   *40*
  The cloudy messenger turns me his back
  And hums, as who should say 'You'll rue the time
  That clogs me with this answer'.

Lennox   And that well might
  Advise him to a caution t' hold what distance
  His wisdom can provide. Some holy angel   *45*
  Fly to the court of England and unfold
  His message ere he come, that a swift blessing
  May soon return to this our suffering country
  Under a hand accurs'd!

Lord   I'll send my prayers with him.

Exeunt

ACT FOUR

The appearance of the witches in Act I, Scene iii, presaged Macbeth's first steps in crime; now he seeks them out and they introduce his deeper and much more desperate involvement in evil.

1. *brinded:* streaked. This cat (perhaps what we should call a tabby) is the First Witch's familiar, called Graymalkin, Act I, Scene i, line 9.

2. *hedge-pig:* hedgehog.

3. *Harpier:* the Third Witch's familiar. This is probably the mythical monster, a harpy, a creature with a woman's face and body and a bird's wings and claws. *Harpier* screams, and the Third Witch announces this as the signal to begin.

6–8. The toad has, while sleeping, sweated poison (*swelter'd venom sleeping got*) for 31 days and nights.

12. A slice of marsh-snake.

16. *fork:* the forked tongue.
blind-worm's sting: we know now that the blind-worm, or slow-worm, is not poisonous, but there was a firm belief in Shakespeare's time that it was.
17. *howlet's wing:* owl's wing.
19. The witch commands the filthy mixture to seethe and gain evil power.

ACT FOUR

SCENE I—*A dark cave. In the middle, a cauldron boiling*

Thunder.   Enter the three WITCHES

First Witch
> Thrice the brinded cat hath mew'd.

Second Witch
> Thrice and once the hedge-pig whin'd.

Third Witch
> Harpier cries; 'tis time, 'tis time.

First Witch
> Round about the cauldron go;
> In the poison'd entrails throw.   5
> Toad that under cold stone
> Days and nights has thirty-one
> Swelter'd venom sleeping got
> Boil thou first i th' charmed pot.

All
> Double, double toil and trouble;   10
> Fire burn, and cauldron bubble.

Second Witch
> Fillet of a fenny snake,
> In the cauldron boil and bake;
> Eye of newt, and toe of frog,
> Wool of bat, and tongue of dog,   15
> Adder's fork, and blind-worm's sting,
> Lizard's leg, and howlet's wing—
> For a charm of pow'rful trouble,
> Like a hell-broth boil and bubble.

All
> Double, double toil and trouble;   20
> Fire burn, and cauldron bubble.

23. *Witch's mummy:* dried flesh from a witch's body. (Dried human flesh was thought to have medicinal and magical powers.)
maw and gulf: throat and stomach.
24. *ravin'd:* stuffed with the flesh of its human victim.
25. The hemlock plant is in any case poisonous; digging it up at night was supposed to increase its powers.
26–31. The Jew, the Turk, the Tartar and the baby strangled at birth would all be anti-Christian or non-Christian, and certainly unchristened.
27. *slips of yew:* cuttings from a yew-tree, which is associated with churchyards and is also poisonous (cattle sometimes become ill through eating yew-leaves).
28. Cut off during an eclipse of the moon (a time of ill-omen to the superstitious).
31. Born to a prostitute, in a ditch.
32. *gruel:* a soupy mixture.
slab: slimy and sticky.
33. *tiger's chaudron:* a tiger's guts.
34. *ingredience:* we would write 'ingredients'.

39–43. It is unlikely that these lines and stage directions are by Shakespeare.

44. There is an old superstition that sudden unexpected pains are omens of coming events.

Third Witch

>Scale of dragon, tooth of wolf,
>Witch's mummy, maw and gulf
>Of the ravin'd salt-sea shark,
>Root of hemlock digg'd i' th' dark,   25
>Liver of blaspheming Jew,
>Gall of goat, and slips of yew
>Sliver'd in the moon's eclipse,
>Nose of Turk, and Tartar's lips,
>Finger of birth-strangled babe   30
>Ditch-deliver'd by a drab—
>Make the gruel thick and slab;
>Add thereto a tiger's chaudron,
>For th' ingredience of our cauldron.

All

>Double, double toil and trouble;   35
>Fire burn, and cauldron bubble.

Second Witch

>Cool it with a baboon's blood,
>Then the charm is firm and good.

Enter HECATE

Hecate

>O well done! I commend your pains;
>And every one shall share i' th' gains.   40
>And now about the cauldron sing,
>Like elves and fairies in a ring,
>Enchanting all that you put in.
>[*Music and a song:* 'Black Spirits, etc.' *Exit* HECATE]

Second Witch

>By the pricking of my thumbs,
>Something wicked this way comes. [*Knocking*]   45
>Open, locks, whoever knocks.

Enter MACBETH

Macbeth

>How now, you secret, black, and midnight hags!

48. *A deed . . . name:* It's too horrible to be described.

49. I call upon you in the name of your devilish art.

51–2. *let them fight . . . churches:* again, the anti-Christian nature of witchcraft is emphasized.
52. *yesty:* frothing, like fermenting yeast.
53. *swallow navigation up:* wreck ships.
54. *Though bladed corn be lodg'd:* though the corn is blown flat even before the ears are formed.

55. *their warders' heads:* the heads of those who guard them.

56–7. *slope . . . foundations:* bend down to their bases, i.e. are blown flat.
57–8. *though . . . together:* Macbeth's selfish preoccupation has now gone to extremes. He has reached the desperate state of a crazy dictator who doesn't mind if the universe is destroyed as long as he gets his own way.
nature's germens: the very seeds of life.
59. *till destruction sicken:* destruction is personified as a violent man who finally becomes repelled by his own deeds, like one who eats so much that he makes himself sick.

62. *our masters:* the devils whom the witches serve; it is they who now take the forms of the apparitions.

64. *farrow:* piglets (the number 9 – 3 times 3 – was specially potent in magic).
sweaten: sweated, oozed out.
65. *gibbet:* gallows.

67. Show yourself, and at the same time go through your performance efficiently.
Stage Direction The *Armed Head* must be the helmeted head of Macbeth as it is when Macduff strikes it off later. At present it has no special meaning for Macbeth (*thou unknown power*, line 68).

What is't you do?
All   A deed without a name.
Macbeth
  I conjure you by that which you profess—
  Howe'er you come to know it—answer me.   *50*
  Though you untie the winds and let them fight
  Against the churches; though the yesty waves
  Confound and swallow navigation up;
  Though bladed corn be lodg'd and trees blown
      down;
  Though castles topple on their warders' heads;   *55*
  Though palaces and pyramids do slope
  Their heads to their foundations; though the treasure
  Of nature's germens tumble all together,
  Even till destruction sicken—answer me
  To what I ask you.
First Witch   Speak.
Second Witch   Demand.
Third Witch   We'll answer.   *60*
First Witch
  Say, if thou'dst rather hear it from our mouths,
  Or from our masters?
Macbeth   Call 'em; let me see 'em.
First Witch
  Pour in sow's blood that hath eaten
  Her nine farrow; grease that's sweaten
  From the murderer's gibbet throw   *65*
  Into the flame.
All   Come, high or low;
  Thyself and office deftly show.

    Thunder. FIRST APPARITION, *an Armed Head*

Macbeth
  Tell me, thou unknown power—
First Witch   He knows thy thought.
  Hear his speech, but say thou nought.

73. *harp'd:* guessed.
Stage Direction The *Bloody Child* is Macduff as a baby *from his mother's womb untimely ripp'd* (Act V, Scene viii, lines 15–16).

77. *Had I three ears . . . :* Macbeth's grim humour suggests that he retains some of his old confidence; later he declines into a state of hopelessness and apathy.

83. *take a bond of fate:* hold Fate itself to its word, by killing Macduff.

84. So that I can prove that my weak fears are unjustified.

85. He hears the thunder of the Stage Direction as he speaks. Thunder was often regarded as the voice of an angry god.
Stage Direction The *Child Crowned* is Malcolm, who later orders his troops to use branches from Birnam Wood as camouflage.

86. *issue:* child.

87–8. *round And top:* a very Shakespearian phrase, full of meaning. A crown is literally round and is worn on top of the head, but also (especially in Macbeth's eyes) it is metaphorically the 'rounding-off' and summit of all ambition.

Apparition
  Macbeth! Macbeth! Macbeth! Beware Macduff;   70
  Beware the Thane of Fife. Dismiss me. Enough.

                    He descends

Macbeth
  Whate'er thou art, for thy good caution, thanks;
  Thou hast harp'd my fear aright. But one word more—
First Witch
  He will not be commanded. Here's another,
  More potent than the first.   75

      Thunder. SECOND APPARITION, *a Bloody Child*

Apparition
  Macbeth! Macbeth! Macbeth!
Macbeth
  Had I three ears, I'd hear thee.
Apparition
  Be bloody, bold, and resolute; laugh to scorn
  The pow'r of man, for none of woman born
  Shall harm Macbeth.   [*Descends*]   80
Macbeth
  Then live, Macduff; what need I fear of thee?
  But yet I'll make assurance double sure
  And take a bond of fate. Thou shalt not live;
  That I may tell pale-hearted fear it lies,
  And sleep in spite of thunder.

      Thunder. THIRD APPARITION, *a Child Crowned,*
              with a tree in his hand

                          What is this   85
  That rises like the issue of a king,
  And wears upon his baby brow the round
  And top of sovereignty?
All   Listen, but speak not to't.
Apparition
  Be lion-mettled, proud, and take no care

                        139

90. *Who chafes, who frets:* who rages and storms.

92. Birnam and Dunsinane are about twelve miles apart. You may think that Shakespeare gives the impression that they are much closer than this in Act V.

93. *That will never be:* Macbeth takes the apparitions' words very literally and unquestioningly. Perhaps he simply dares not take them otherwise?

94. *impress:* conscript, i.e. make the trees march.

95. *bodements:* prophecies.

96. *Rebellion's head:* the forces which may rise to unseat Macbeth from the throne. Possibly he is thinking specifically of the *First Apparition.*

98. *Shall live the lease of nature:* the full term of human life.

98–9. *pay his breath . . . custom:* stop breathing in the course of time, i.e. die a natural death.

101–2. After a show of returning confidence Macbeth cannot resist asking the question that Fleance's escape has strengthened in his mind; 'Have I committed these crimes merely for another man's sons to inherit the throne?'

Stage Direction *Hautboys:* the hautboy was a high-pitched wooden instrument, as the name suggests. The modern form of the word is 'oboe'.

105. *noise:* music.

Stage Direction *A Show of eight Kings:* a dumb-show, or mime, was a regular feature in plays of Shakespeare's time. In this one Banquo mocks Macbeth by introducing him to a line of eight Stuart kings all descendants of his. This seems to be roughly historically accurate, except that there is no mention of Mary, Queen of Scots. During the show Macbeth goes through a variety of strong emotions, horror, rage, despair and finally blank depression.

112. *thy hair:* This probably means 'your general appearance or character'.

Who chafes, who frets, or where conspirers are: *90*
Macbeth shall never vanquish'd be until
Great Birnam wood to high Dunsinane Hill
Shall come against him.   [*Descends*]
Macbeth   That will never be.
Who can impress the forest, bid the tree
Unfix his earth-bound root? Sweet bodements, good! *95*
Rebellion's head rise never till the wood
Of Birnam rise, and our high-plac'd Macbeth
Shall live the lease of nature, pay his breath
To time and mortal custom. Yet my heart
Throbs to know one thing; tell me, if your art   *100*
Can tell so much—shall Banquo's issue ever
Reign in this kingdom?
All   Seek to know no more.
Macbeth
I will be satisfied. Deny me this,
And an eternal curse fall on you! Let me know.
Why sinks that cauldron? And what noise is this?   *105*

Hautboys

First Witch
Show!
Second Witch
Show!
Third Witch
Show!
All
Show his eyes, and grieve his heart;
Come like shadows, so depart!   *110*

A Show of eight Kings, and BANQUO *last; the last
king with a glass in his hand*

Macbeth
Thou art too like the spirit of Banquo; down!
Thy crown does sear mine eye-balls. And thy hair,
Thou other gold-bound brow, is like the first.

141

116. *Start, eyes:* Macbeth would rather that his eyes should pop from his head than that he should see any more.

117. *th' crack of doom:* Doomsday, the moment of the 'last trump', when the world will come to an end.

118–20. The mirror carried by the eighth shows Macbeth many Banquo-like figures, including some who carry *two-fold balls* (double orbs representing the union of England and Scotland) and *treble sceptres* (signifying rule over England, Scotland and Ireland). Such a description applied to James I, who was descended from Banquo, and who probably saw the play at some time.

122. *blood-bolter'd:* with blood-plastered hair.

129. *antic round:* grotesque dance.

130–1. It is possible that these words were really addressed to James I seated in the audience or perhaps they are an ironic comment on Macbeth.

132–3. Macbeth is getting into the habit of uttering hideous but empty curses.

134. It is interesting to note that Lennox still serves Macbeth, in spite of his expressed doubts about him in Act III, Scene vi.

137–8. More curses!

A third is like the former. Filthy hags!
Why do you show me this? A fourth? Start, eyes.   *115*
What, will the line stretch out to th' crack of doom?
Another yet? A seventh? I'll see no more.
And yet the eighth appears, who bears a glass
Which shows me many more; and some I see
That two-fold balls and treble sceptres carry.   *120*
Horrible sight! Now I see 'tis true;
For the blood-bolter'd Banquo smiles upon me,
And points at them for his. [*The show vanishes*]
                        What! is this so?

First Witch

Ay, sir, all this is so. But why
Stands Macbeth thus amazedly?   *125*
Come, sisters, cheer we up his sprites,
And show the best of our delights;
I'll charm the air to give a sound,
While you perform your antic round;
That this great king may kindly say,   *130*
Our duties did his welcome pay.

        Music.   *The* WITCHES *dance, and vanish*

Macbeth

Where are they? Gone? Let this pernicious hour
Stand aye accursed in the calendar.
Come in, without there.

                  Enter LENNOX

Lennox   What's your Grace's will?
Macbeth
Saw you the Weird Sisters?
Lennox   No, my lord.   *135*
Macbeth
Came they not by you?
Lennox   No, indeed, my lord.
Macbeth
Infected be the air whereon they ride;

140–1. Macbeth is shocked that the prophecies seem already to be making sense.

143. Time is forestalling him – he was planning to kill Macduff, but he has escaped to England.
144–5. 'The only way of ensuring that an intention becomes a deed is to act as soon as you think of it'. In the next sentence Macbeth resolves to go one better; to act on emotion (*firstlings of my heart*) without thinking purposefully at all.

149. *surprise:* take by surprise.

152. *trace:* follow.

SCENE II

Macduff has fled to England, without even telling his wife. She is naturally bitter about this, and seems to think he is a coward. It is often suggested that he went secretly so that Macbeth would have no excuse for harming his wife and children. Examine the evidence as it comes out and try to decide whether Macduff's action is justifiable. Ross and the Messenger show themselves in this scene as ordinary decent men bewildered under an evil political regime.

3–4. *When our actions . . . traitors:* Lady Macduff thinks that her husband has not actually plotted against Macbeth, but that he has fled through fear and thus laid himself open to the charge of treachery.

And damn'd all those that trust them! I did hear
The galloping of horse. Who was't came by?
Lennox
'Tis two or three, my lord, that bring you word   *140*
Macduff is fled to England.
Macbeth   Fled to England!
Lennox
Ay, my good lord.
Macbeth [*aside*]
Time, thou anticipat'st my dread exploits.
The flighty purpose never is o'ertook
Unless the deed go with it. From this moment   *145*
The very firstlings of my heart shall be
The firstlings of my hand. And even now,
To crown my thoughts with acts, be it thought and done:
The castle of Macduff I will surprise,
Seize upon Fife, give to the edge o' th' sword   *150*
His wife, his babes, and all unfortunate souls
That trace him in his line. No boasting like a fool:
This deed I'll do before this purpose cool.
But no more sights!—Where are these gentlemen?
Come, bring me where they are.   *155*

Exeunt

SCENE II—*Fife. Macduff's castle*

Enter LADY MACDUFF, *her* SON, *and* ROSS

Lady Macduff
What had he done to make him fly the land?
Ross
You must have patience, madam.
Lady Macduff   He had none;
His flight was madness. When our actions do not,
Our fears do make us traitors.
Ross   You know not

7. *titles:* his estates and possessions.

9. *He wants the natural touch:* a terrible accusation from a wife, equivalent to saying 'he hasn't any normal feelings of love and protectiveness'.

10. *most diminutive:* tiniest. This natural image is a striking one – wren versus owl – and it is by no means impossible that a wren would fly aggressively at an owl, if not actually fight it.

12–14. 'His fear for his own skin has driven out all love for his family. What's more, the same fear has driven out all sense, too; what reason is there for such a flight?' This gives Ross his cue to suggest that Macduff may have grimly adequate reasons for fleeing.

coz: an affectionate term, applied in a variety of relationships.

15. *school:* control.

for: as for, concerning.

17. *The fits o' th' season:* the violent disturbances of the time.

18–19. *when we are traitors . . . ourselves:* when we're regarded as traitors without knowing it.

19–20. *When we hold rumour . . . fear:* when we believe the stories we hear, because we're afraid, without knowing what there is to be afraid of.

22. *Each way and none:* the general idea seems to be that frightened people are tossed backwards and forwards on the sea of fear without getting anywhere.

24–5. Ross's sage remark suggests to the audience that some change in fortune may be about to occur. This idea is underlined by the sea metaphor which could well represent the moment just before the tide changes.

28–9. Ross means that he feels like crying and would embarrass Lady Macduff by doing so if he stayed any longer.

30–63. Macduff's small son, with his precocious questions and answers, provides an interval of partly comic Shakespearian 'back-chat' which accentuates the horror of the end of the scene. There is, of course, pathos too, and the sense that Macbeth is going to take a further step against the natural order of things by killing these helpless people.

30. *Sirrah:* a term used by parents to children (and also by masters to servants).

dead: as good as dead. She doesn't expect to see him again.

Whether it was his wisdom or his fear.   5
Lady Macduff
  Wisdom! To leave his wife, to leave his babes,
  His mansion, and his titles, in a place
  From whence himself does fly? He loves us not;
  He wants the natural touch; for the poor wren,
  The most diminutive of birds, will fight,   10
  Her young ones in her nest, against the owl.
  All is the fear, and nothing is the love;
  As little is the wisdom, where the flight
  So runs against all reason.
Ross   My dearest coz,
  I pray you, school yourself. But, for your husband,   15
  He is noble, wise, judicious, and best knows
  The fits o' th' season. I dare not speak much further;
  But cruel are the times, when we are traitors
  And do not know ourselves; when we hold rumour
  From what we fear, yet know not what we fear,   20
  But float upon a wild and violent sea
  Each way and none. I take my leave of you;
  Shall not be long but I'll be here again.
  Things at the worst will cease, or else climb upward
  To what they were before.—My pretty cousin,   25
  Blessing upon you!
Lady Macduff
  Father'd he is, and yet he's fatherless.
Ross
  I am so much a fool, should I stay longer,
  It would be my disgrace and your discomfort.
  I take my leave at once.

                          Exit

Lady Macduff   Sirrah, your father's dead;   30
  And what will you do now? How will you live?
Son
  As birds do, mother.
Lady Macduff   What, with worms and flies?

34. *lime:* bird-lime, a sticky substance spread to catch birds.

35. *The pitfall . . . the gin:* two other methods of catching birds – a disguised hole in the ground (presumably for flightless birds) and a snare.

36. *Poor birds . . . for:* the boy is saying, shrewdly, 'If I'm a poor bird, as you say, I'm in no danger; no-one's silly enough to set traps for *poor* birds!'

41. *Then you'll buy . . . again:* If they're as easy to get as all that, they won't be worth keeping.

42–3. *Thou speak'st . . . thee:* You're not talking very sensibly – but perhaps sensibly enough, considering how young you are.

45. She is probably referring to her husband's running away and leaving her, which she sees as treachery. In line 47 she suggests that he has broken his marriage-vow by leaving her.

Son

  With what I get, I mean; and so do they.

Lady Macduff

  Poor bird! thou'dst never fear the net nor lime,
  The pitfall nor the gin.   35

Son

  Why should I, mother? Poor birds they are not set for.
  My father is not dead, for all your saying.

Lady Macduff

  Yes, he is dead. How wilt thou do for a father?

Son

  Nay, how will you do for a husband?

Lady Macduff

  Why, I can buy me twenty at any market.   40

Son

  Then you'll buy 'em to sell again.

Lady Macduff

  Thou speak'st with all thy wit; and yet, i' faith,
  With wit enough for thee.

Son

  Was my father a traitor, mother?

Lady Macduff

  Ay, that he was.   45

Son

  What is a traitor?

Lady Macduff

  Why, one that swears and lies.

Son

  And be all traitors that do so?

Lady Macduff

  Every one that does so is a traitor, and must be
  hang'd.   50

Son

  And must they all be hang'd that swear and lie?

Lady Macduff

  Every one.

56. *enow:* enough.

58. *poor monkey!* an affectionate phrase, showing her amusement at her son's clever chatter. But immediately after it she becomes sad and serious again.

64. Ross's warnings were vague, this Messenger's much more urgent. The pace of the scene changes abruptly.
65. *Though in your state . . . perfect:* Although I know your honourable status very well.
66. *I doubt:* I am afraid.
67. *homely:* humble.

69–70. 'It is cruel of me to frighten you in this way; to do worse to you would be monstrous'. He makes it plain in the next line that someone is likely to *do worse* to her soon.

74–6. *where to do harm . . . folly:* 'where doing harm often receives praise, and doing good is regarded as dangerous and stupid'. The complete upset of values under Macbeth's tyranny is plainly stated.

Son

    Who must hang them?

Lady Macduff

    Why, the honest men.

Son

    Then the liars and swearers are fools; for there are   55
    liars and swearers enow to beat the honest men and
    hang up them.

Lady Macduff

    Now, God help thee, poor monkey! But how wilt
    thou do for a father?

Son

    If he were dead, you'd weep for him; if you would not,   60
    it were a good sign that I should quickly have a new
    father.

Lady Macduff

    Poor prattler, how thou talk'st!

Enter a MESSENGER

Messenger

    Bless you, fair dame! I am not to you known,
    Though in your state of honour I am perfect.   65
    I doubt some danger does approach you nearly.
    If you will take a homely man's advice,
    Be not found here; hence, with your little ones.
    To fright you thus, methinks, I am too savage;
    To do worse to you were fell cruelty,   70
    Which is too nigh your person. Heaven preserve you!
    I dare abide no longer.

Exit

Lady Macduff   Whither should I fly?
    I have done no harm. But I remember now
    I am in this earthly world, where to do harm
    Is often laudable, to do good sometime   75
    Accounted dangerous folly. Why then, alas,
    Do I put up that womanly defence

79–84. Mother and son both forget recent cynical comments about Macduff and oppose Macbeth's hired thugs bravely.

82. *shag-ear'd:* if this is the word Shakespeare actually wrote (which is doubtful) it probably means 'with hair sprouting from the ears' – the kind of thing a child might well notice.

82–3. *egg* and *fry:* These are contemptuous terms applied to Lady Macduff's son because of his youthfulness and small stature.

fry: baby fish.

SCENE III

The dictator, Macbeth, now has a firm hold on Scotland. Malcolm, in the safety of the English court, naturally suspects anyone who comes from Scotland to persuade him to go back there. He tests Macduff's honesty in an elaborate way (possibly too elaborate?).

The scene contrasts the miseries of life under a cruel tyrant with the happiness of life under a holy king.

1–2. Here, and for some time afterwards, Malcolm seems to indicate that he has no hope and can only accept the situation passively. Macduff, on the other hand, urges active opposition to Macbeth.

3. *the mortal sword:* the sword that kills.

4. *Bestride . . . birthdom:* defend our native country in its misfortune, as one might stand protectively over a fallen comrade.

5–8. *new sorrows . . . dolour:* woeful cries at fresh miseries are a blow (a 'slap in the face') to the forces of goodness. Heaven echoes with similar (*Like*) wails, in sympathy with Scotland. (The audience will recall the recent cries of Lady Macduff and her son, at this point.)

8. *wail:* bewail, lament.

8–17. Malcolm replies cautiously, almost as though he is saying; 'I regret any unhappiness that can be proved to have occurred, and I'll put right anything I can, if a suitable time (*time to friend*) comes.' Then he quite openly expresses his doubts about Macduff (lines 12–13); 'People once believed what Macbeth said—and you have shown respect and loyalty to him in the past. What's more, it's suspicious that he hasn't harmed you. I may seem gullible, but I can see that you might win favour with Macbeth by harming me. It might be expedient to sacrifice a helpless creature (like me) to placate him.'

To say I have done no harm?

Enter MURDERERS

                What are these faces?

First Murderer
  Where is your husband?
Lady Macduff
  I hope, in no place so unsanctified   *80*
  Where such as thou mayst find him.
First Murderer   He's a traitor.
Son
  Thou liest, thou shag-ear'd villain.
First Murderer   What, you egg?

          [*stabbing him*]

  Young fry of treachery!
Son   He has kill'd me, mother.
  Run away, I pray you.

      Dies.   Exit LADY MACDUFF, *crying 'Murder!'*

SCENE III—*England.   Before King Edward's palace*

Enter MALCOLM *and* MACDUFF

Malcolm
  Let us seek out some desolate shade, and there
  Weep our sad bosoms empty.
Macduff   Let us rather
  Hold fast the mortal sword, and like good men
  Bestride our down-fall'n birthdom. Each new morn
  New widows howl, new orphans cry; new sorrows   *5*
  Strike heaven on the face, that it resounds
  As if it felt with Scotland and yell'd out
  Like syllable of dolour.
Malcolm   What I believe, I'll wail;
  What know, believe; and what I can redress,

18. No doubt Macduff protests violently at these charges.

19–20. *A good . . . charge:* even a good man may falter and step back (into evil ways) when a king gives the orders.

21. *transpose:* change. Malcolm means 'You are what you are; my suspicions of you won't make you vicious'.

22. *the brightest:* Lucifer, who turned against God, led the revolt in Heaven, was defeated and thrown down (see, particularly, Milton's *Paradise Lost*, Book II).

23–4. Dr. Johnson paraphrased these lines as follows: 'I do not say that your virtuous appearance proves you a traitor, for virtue must wear its proper form, though that form be counterfeited by villainy'.

25. The thought in Malcolm's mind seems to be that perhaps Macbeth promised Macduff that his family would be left unharmed if he betrayed Malcolm.

26. *rawness:* unprotected state.

29–31. 'Don't let my suspicions alone dishonour you. I'm simply protecting myself by voicing them'. He ends, apologetically, by saying that Macduff may very well be an honest man, in spite of these suspicions.

33. *For goodness . . . thee:* Macduff bitterly accuses Malcolm of being too feeble to oppose Macbeth.

33–4. *Wear thou . . . affeer'd:* (addressing Macbeth) go on enjoying the fruits of your crimes; you're undisputed master now.

affeer'd: a legal term meaning 'confirmed'.

34. Macduff gives up the attempt and turns to go. But Malcolm has by no means completed his testing yet.

37. The Elizabethans thought of the East as the main source of gold and precious stones.

to boot: as well.

39. *sinks beneath the yoke:* The country is like an ill-treated animal pulling a heavy load.

As I shall find the time to friend, I will.   10
What you have spoke, it may be so perchance.
This tyrant, whose sole name blisters our tongues,
Was once thought honest; you have lov'd him well;
He hath not touch'd you yet. I am young; but something
You may deserve of him through me; and wisdom   15
To offer up a weak, poor, innocent lamb
T' appease an angry god.
Macduff
I am not treacherous.
Malcolm   But Macbeth is.
A good and virtuous nature may recoil
In an imperial charge. But I shall crave your pardon; 20
That which you are, my thoughts cannot transpose;
Angels are bright still, though the brightest fell.
Though all things foul would wear the brows of grace,
Yet grace must still look so.
Macduff   I have lost my hopes.
Malcolm
Perchance even there where I did find my doubts.   25
Why in that rawness left you wife and child,
Those precious motives, those strong knots of love,
Without leave-taking? I pray you,
Let not my jealousies be your dishonours,
But mine own safeties. You may be rightly just,   30
Whatever I shall think.
Macduff   Bleed, bleed, poor country.
Great tyranny, lay thou thy basis sure,
For goodness dare not check thee. Wear thou thy wrongs,
The title is affeer'd. Fare thee well, lord.
I would not be the villain that thou think'st   35
For the whole space that's in the tyrant's grasp
And the rich East to boot.
Malcolm   Be not offended.
I speak not as in absolute fear of you.
I think our country sinks beneath the yoke;
It weeps, it bleeds; and each new day a gash   40

41. *withal:* moreover.

42. That people would support my cause.

43. *gracious England:* King Edward the Confessor, who has God's grace.

44. From this point onwards Malcolm deliberately paints a frightful portrait of himself. He wants to see if Macduff would have him as king, however evil he is; if so, then his suspicions are proved to be correct – Macduff has come to trap him.

for all this: in spite of all this.

51. *particulars:* detailed varieties.

grafted: incorporated, like a graft in gardening (the metaphor is followed up in the next line by the word *open'd* – like the bud of an evil-looking flower).

54–5. *Esteem him . . . harms:* Judge Macbeth to be as innocent as a lamb, in contrast with my unlimited (*confineless*) vices.

58. *Luxurious:* lustful.

avaricious: miserly.

There is no evidence that Macbeth has either of these faults, but Malcolm is now presenting a kind of 'fantasy Macbeth', the sum of all evils, in order to declare himself even worse!

59. *Sudden:* violent.

smacking: tasting.

60–1. *but . . . voluptuousness:* my lustfulness has no limit. The *cistern* (line 63) is what has no bottom.

63–5. *my desire . . . my will:* my lust would overcome all restraints to satisfy itself.

66. We may imagine Macduff being silent for a few moments, not knowing what to say to such an astonishing piece of self-condemnation. Then he admits that lustfulness has been the downfall of many rulers; nevertheless, even this may not rule Malcolm out as an improvement upon Macbeth as King of Scotland.

70–2. You may satisfy all your sexual desires lavishly in secret, preserving a reputation for self-control, by deceiving everyone.

Is added to her wounds. I think withal
There would be hands uplifted in my right;
And here, from gracious England, have I offer
Of goodly thousands. But, for all this,
When I shall tread upon the tyrant's head,   45
Or wear it on my sword, yet my poor country
Shall have more vices than it had before;
More suffer, and more sundry ways than ever,
By him that shall succeed.
Macduff   What should he be?
Malcolm
It is myself I mean; in whom I know   50
All the particulars of vice so grafted
That, when they shall be open'd, black Macbeth
Will seem as pure as snow; and the poor state
Esteem him as a lamb, being compar'd
With my confineless harms.
Macduff   Not in the legions   55
Of horrid hell can come a devil more damn'd
In evils to top Macbeth.
Malcolm   I grant him bloody,
Luxurious, avaricious, false, deceitful,
Sudden, malicious, smacking of every sin
That has a name; but there's no bottom, none,   60
In my voluptuousness. Your wives, your daughters,
Your matrons, and your maids, could not fill up
The cistern of my lust; and my desire
All continent impediments would o'erbear
That did oppose my will. Better Macbeth   65
Than such an one to reign.
Macduff   Boundless intemperance
In nature is a tyranny; it hath been
Th' untimely emptying of the happy throne
And fall of many kings. But fear not yet
To take upon you what is yours. You may   70
Convey your pleasures in a spacious plenty,
And yet seem cold, the time you may so hoodwink.

73–6. That ravenous creature, your lust, can't possibly take as many women as are willing to offer themselves to a king, when they see his inclination.

76–84. Malcolm now moves on to the second major vice he accuses himself of – greed for possessions (*avarice*).
77. *ill-compos'd affection:* unbalanced temperament.
78. *stanchless:* uncontrollable.
79. *cut off:* kill.
80. *his:* one nobleman's.

82–3. *that I should . . . unjust:* make up false grievances (as excuses for robbing them).

86–9. *summer-seeming:* Macduff's point is that lust isn't likely to last throughout a man's life (it will pass, like summer), but avarice is different, and worse. Even so, Scotland can probably cope with this, too.
88. *foisons:* plentiful resources.
89. *Of your mere own:* out of what really belongs to you (as king).
portable: bearable.

92. *verity:* truthfulness.
93. *Bounty:* generosity.

95. *I have no relish of them:* I haven't a scrap of any of these in me.
96. In variations of every possible sin.
97–100. This is just the kind of conclusive, all-embracingly destructive threat that Macbeth makes at his most desperate moments (see, e.g., Act IV, Scene i, lines 57–60). Malcolm still seems to be using the tyrant as his model of wickedness.
98. *concord:* harmony.
99. *Uproar:* throw into chaos.

102. Macduff has now had enough, and gives up the attempt to persuade Malcolm.

We have willing dames enough; there cannot be
That vulture in you to devour so many
As will to greatness dedicate themselves,   *75*
Finding it so inclin'd.

Malcolm   With this there grows
In my most ill-compos'd affection such
A stanchless avarice that, were I King,
I should cut off the nobles for their lands,
Desire his jewels, and this other's house;   *80*
And my more-having would be as a sauce
To make me hunger more, that I should forge
Quarrels unjust against the good and loyal,
Destroying them for wealth.

Macduff   This avarice
Sticks deeper, grows with more pernicious root   *85*
Than summer-seeming lust; and it hath been
The sword of our slain kings. Yet do not fear;
Scotland hath foisons to fill up your will
Of your mere own. All these are portable,
With other graces weigh'd.   *90*

Malcolm
But I have none. The king-becoming graces,
As justice, verity, temp'rance, stableness,
Bounty, perseverance, mercy, lowliness,
Devotion, patience, courage, fortitude,
I have no relish of them; but abound   *95*
In the division of each several crime,
Acting it many ways. Nay, had I pow'r, I should
Pour the sweet milk of concord into hell,
Uproar the universal peace, confound
All unity on earth.

Macduff   O Scotland, Scotland!   *100*

Malcolm
If such a one be fit to govern, speak.
I am as I have spoken.

Macduff   Fit to govern!
No, not to live! O nation miserable,

104. *untitled:* not entitled to the throne.

107. *interdiction:* condemnation.

108. *blaspheme his breed:* disgrace his family.

111. *Died every day she liv'd:* she was so devout that she lived every day as if it were her last.

112–13. *These evils . . . Hath:* we now regard *Hath* as a singular verb, but it was often used with a plural subject in Shakespeare's time.

113. *breast:* heart (thought to be the source of feelings).

115. *Child of integrity:* i.e. 'which was inspired by your honest nature'. Malcolm is now satisfied that Macduff is not acting a sinister part.

116. *black scruples:* dark suspicions.

118. *trains:* tricks, schemes.

119–20. *and modest wisdom . . . haste:* commonsense has prevented me from believing things too easily.

120–1. Malcolm's appeal to divine power, putting fears and doubts away in the process, is in line with the feeling of the remainder of the play. God's grace is sought by the human forces of goodness in the struggle to defeat Macbeth, the man committed to the service of the powers of evil.

123. *Unspeak mine own detraction:* take back the things I accused myself of.

abjure: deny.

125. *For strangers . . . nature:* as qualities quite foreign to me.

126. *Unknown to woman:* virginal.

never was forsworn: never dishonoured by being false.

127. Far from being avaricious, Malcolm declares he doesn't particularly prize his own possessions, let alone covet those of others.

135. *at a point:* fully prepared for action.

136–7. *the chance of goodness . . . quarrel!* A typically concentrated Shakespearian statement, meaning something like 'may our chances of success be as great as the justice of our cause'.

138–9. It is not hard to sympathize with Macduff's bewilderment. But could Malcolm have tested him in any more effective way?

With an untitled tyrant bloody-scept'red,
When shalt thou see thy wholesome days again,   *105*
Since that the truest issue of thy throne
By his own interdiction stands accurs'd
And does blaspheme his breed? Thy royal father
Was a most sainted king; the queen that bore thee,
Oft'ner upon her knees than on her feet,   *110*
Died every day she liv'd. Fare thee well!
These evils thou repeat'st upon thyself
Hath banish'd me from Scotland. O my breast,
Thy hope ends here!

Malcolm   Macduff, this noble passion,
Child of integrity, hath from my soul   *115*
Wip'd the black scruples, reconcil'd my thoughts
To thy good truth and honour. Devilish Macbeth
By many of these trains hath sought to win me
Into his power; and modest wisdom plucks me
From over-credulous haste. But God above   *120*
Deal between thee and me; for even now
I put myself to thy direction, and
Unspeak mine own detraction, here abjure
The taints and blames I laid upon myself
For strangers to my nature. I am yet   *125*
Unknown to woman, never was forsworn,
Scarcely have coveted what was mine own,
At no time broke my faith, would not betray
The devil to his fellow, and delight
No less in truth than life. My first false speaking   *130*
Was this upon myself. What I am truly
Is thine and my poor country's to command:
Whither indeed, before thy here-approach,
Old Siward with ten thousand warlike men
Already at a point was setting forth.   *135*
Now we'll together; and the chance of goodness
Be like our warranted quarrel! Why are you silent?

Macduff
Such welcome and unwelcome things at once

140-59. In this passage Edward the Confessor is presented as a source of healing. He can heal not only the glandular disease, scrofula (the tradition that English sovereigns possessed this power continued until at least Queen Anne's time), but also implicitly he can heal political and social evils, like Macbeth's régime. It is Edward's soldiers that make it possible for Malcolm to return powerfully to Scotland.

142. *stay his cure:* wait for him to cure them.

142-3. *convinces . . . art:* defeats all the skill of trained doctors.

145. *presently amend:* immediately get better.

146. Scrofula is often called 'the King's Evil'.

149. *solicits heaven:* secures help from God.

150. *strangely-visited:* horribly afflicted.

152. *mere:* sheer.

153. *stamp:* coin.

155-6. His successors on the throne will inherit his blessed healing power.

160. Apparently Malcolm sees that Ross is wearing Scottish clothes, but does not at first recognize the man, although he certainly knows him (see Act I, Scene vi). Perhaps he is again suspicious of a visitor from Scotland, until Macduff greets him warmly.

'Tis hard to reconcile.

Enter a DOCTOR

Malcolm
Well; more anon. Comes the King forth, I pray you? *140*
Doctor
Ay, sir. There are a crew of wretched souls
That stay his cure. Their malady convinces
The great assay of art; but at his touch,
Such sanctity hath heaven given his hand,
They presently amend.
Malcolm   I thank you, doctor. *145*

Exit DOCTOR

Macduff
What's the disease he means?
Malcolm   'Tis called the evil:
A most miraculous work in this good king,
Which often since my here-remain in England
I have seen him do. How he solicits heaven,
Himself best knows; but strangely-visited people, *150*
All swoln and ulcerous, pitiful to the eye,
The mere despair of surgery, he cures,
Hanging a golden stamp about their necks,
Put on with holy prayers; and 'tis spoken,
To the succeeding royalty he leaves *155*
The healing benediction. With this strange virtue,
He hath a heavenly gift of prophecy;
And sundry blessings hang about his throne
That speak him full of grace.

Enter ROSS

Macduff   See, who comes here?
Malcolm
My countryman; but yet I know him not. *160*
Macduff
My ever gentle cousin, welcome hither.

163

162. *betimes:* quickly.

163. The things (such as a foul dictatorship) which make men suspicious of each other.

166-7. *nothing . . . knows nothing:* no-one except the most ignorant person (e.g. an imbecile).

168. *rent:* rend, in modern English.

169. *Are made, not mark'd:* uttered, but not noticed (because agonized cries are so common).

170. *A modern ecstasy:* a familiar emotion, something like 'a fashionable disease'.

170-1. *the dead man's knell . . . for who:* people hardly bother to ask who's dead when they hear the bell tolling.

173. 'Dying before they fall ill' – probably because so many are being 'liquidated' by Macbeth's agents.

173-4. *O, relation . . . true!* Your account is too full of horrid detail, but undeniably true.

175. Any news an hour old earns the teller hisses (because it's stale. Evil things are happening all the time).

176. *teems:* gives birth to.

176-240. In the rest of the scene Ross finds it difficult to break the news of the slaughter of Macduff's family, and when he does so Macduff is at first almost struck dumb with horror. Only when he expresses his feelings of sorrow and anger can he cope with the dreadful event. Then he is ready to seek a righteous revenge.

179. *well at peace:* There is something unacceptable to us in a pun at such a time; but it does convey Ross's uneasiness.

180. *a niggard of your speech:* so reluctant to speak.

181-3. *the tidings:* These seem to be the news of the death of Lady Macduff and her children.
rumour: This must be of a general uprising against Macbeth.
were out: had left their homes to oppose Macbeth.

Malcolm

  I know him now. Good God betimes remove
  The means that makes us strangers!

Ross   Sir, amen.

Macduff

  Stands Scotland where it did?

Ross   Alas, poor country,

  Almost afraid to know itself! It cannot   *165*
  Be call'd our mother, but our grave; where nothing,
  But who knows nothing, is once seen to smile;
  Where sighs, and groans, and shrieks, that rent the air,
  Are made, not mark'd; where violent sorrow seems
  A modern ecstasy; the dead man's knell   *170*
  Is there scarce ask'd for who; and good men's lives
  Expire before the flowers in their caps,
  Dying or ere they sicken.

Macduff   O, relation

  Too nice, and yet too true!

Malcolm   What's the newest grief?

Ross

  That of an hour's age doth hiss the speaker: *175*
  Each minute teems a new one.

Macduff   How does my wife?

Ross

  Why, well.

Macduff   And all my children?

Ross   Well too.

Macduff

  The tyrant has not batter'd at their peace?

Ross

  No; they were well at peace when I did leave 'em.

Macduff

  Be not a niggard of your speech. How goes't?   *180*

Ross

  When I came hither to transport the tidings,
  Which I have heavily borne, there ran a rumour
  Of many worthy fellows that were out;

185. *the tyrant's power afoot:* Macbeth's army mobilized.

186. *your eye . . . :* Ross has turned from Macduff, only too glad to avoid conversation with him, and is addressing Malcolm.

188. *To doff . . . distresses:* To get rid of their troubles, as though throwing off clothes.

189. Exactly the same phrase was used of King Edward in line 43.

191. *older:* more experienced.

192. *gives out:* proclaims.

195. *Where hearing . . . them:* Where they wouldn't be heard by anyone. *latch:* catch.

196–7. *a fee-grief . . . breast?* a sorrow belonging to one particular person.

197–8. *No mind . . . some woe:* All decent people feel sympathy for those who suffer, and thus suffer themselves.

202. *possess them:* inform them.

205–7. *To relate . . . death of you:* To tell you in detail how it happened would add your death to the deaths of those you loved.

206. *quarry:* means a heap of animals killed in hunting, and *deer* is a deeply sympathetic pun on 'dear'.

208–9. Macduff has tried not to show his feelings to the others, by hiding his face. Malcolm knows that he must express what he feels (*Give sorrow words . . .*).

210. *o'erfraught:* overburdened.

Which was to my belief witness'd the rather
For that I saw the tyrant's power afoot.   *185*
Now is the time of help; your eye in Scotland
Would create soldiers, make our women fight,
To doff their dire distresses.
Malcolm   Be't their comfort
We are coming thither. Gracious England hath
Lent us good Siward and ten thousand men—   *190*
An older and a better soldier none
That Christendom gives out.
Ross   Would I could answer
This comfort with the like! But I have words
That would be howl'd out in the desert air,
Where hearing should not latch them.
Macduff   What concern they? *195*
The general cause, or is it a fee-grief
Due to some single breast?
Ross   No mind that's honest
But in it shares some woe, though the main part
Pertains to you alone.
Macduff   If it be mine,
Keep it not from me; quickly let me have it.   *200*
Ross
Let not your ears despise my tongue for ever,
Which shall possess them with the heaviest sound
That ever yet they heard.
Macduff   Humph! I guess at it.
Ross
Your castle is surpris'd; your wife and babes
Savagely slaughter'd. To relate the manner,   *205*
Were, on the quarry of these murder'd deer,
To add the death of you.
Malcolm   Merciful heaven!
What, man! Ne'er pull your hat upon your brows;
Give sorrow words. The grief that does not speak
Whispers the o'erfraught heart and bids it break.   *210*

212. *And I must . . . thence!* And I had to be absent at the time!

216. *He has no children:* There are several possible explanations of this remark, the most likely being that it is addressed to Macbeth and means that Macduff cannot take an appropriate revenge ('tit for tat'). It might, alternatively, be addressed to Ross referring to Malcolm who doesn't yet know what it is to have a father's feelings.

217. *hell-kite:* a devilish bird of prey, raiding a chicken-run and killing all the birds.

218. *dam:* mother.

222. *things:* beings (i.e. Lady Macduff and the children).

225. *nought:* evil.

226–7. *Not for their own . . . souls:* 'They died because of my sinfulness, not their own'. Macduff sees his personal disaster as the consequence of his own sins, but he is probably not blaming himself for having left his family in Scotland – that was an unfortunate necessity.

228. *whetstone:* a piece of stone on which knives (and swords) are sharpened.

229. *blunt not . . . it:* don't tone down your feelings; express them in full force.

230–1. Macduff declares that he could easily act like a woman (by weeping) or like a boaster (by merely saying what he will do); instead, he intends to return to Scotland and get his revenge.

232. *Cut short all intermission:* cut out all delay.

front to front: face to face.

235. *Heaven forgive him too!* He means that if Macbeth escapes with his life it will mean that he, Macduff, has first forgiven him.

Macduff
  My children too?
Ross   Wife, children, servants, all
  That could be found.
Macduff   And I must be from thence!
  My wife kill'd too?
Ross   I have said.
Malcolm   Be comforted.
  Let's make us med'cines of our great revenge
  To cure this deadly grief.   *215*
Macduff
  He has no children. All my pretty ones?
  Did you say all? O hell-kite! All?
  What, all my pretty chickens and their dam
  At one fell swoop?
Malcolm
  Dispute it like a man.
Macduff   I shall do so;   *220*
  But I must also feel it as a man.
  I cannot but remember such things were
  That were most precious to me. Did heaven look on,
  And would not take their part? Sinful Macduff,
  They were all struck for thee—naught that I am;   *225*
  Not for their own demerits, but for mine,
  Fell slaughter on their souls. Heaven rest them now!
Malcolm
  Be this the whetstone of your sword. Let grief
  Convert to anger; blunt not the heart, enrage it.
Macduff
  O, I could play the woman with mine eyes   *230*
  And braggart with my tongue! But, gentle heavens,
  Cut short all intermission; front to front
  Bring thou this fiend of Scotland and myself;
  Within my sword's length set him; if he scape,
  Heaven forgive him too!

235. *This tune goes manly:* This is a proper, manly way of speaking.

237. *Our lack . . . leave:* The only thing left to do is to say our farewells.

237–9. *Macbeth . . . their instruments:* Macbeth is compared to a ripe fruit which is ready to fall. Perhaps Shakespeare is thinking of the prophecy of the fall of the city of Nineveh in the Bible, where ripe fig-trees symbolized 'strong cities' about to surrender (*Nahum*, iii, 12).

238–9. *the pow'rs above . . . instruments:* he means that God has selected them as the agents of divine vengeance.

240. He implies that dawn will soon break. After the personal crisis of the scene it does look as though the fortunes of all good, true men in Scottish society are about to change.

Malcolm   This tune goes manly.   235
  Come, go we to the King. Our power is ready;
  Our lack is nothing but our leave. Macbeth
  Is ripe for shaking, and the pow'rs above
  Put on their instruments. Receive what cheer you may;
  The night is long that never finds the day.   240

Exeunt

ACT FIVE

SCENE I

We have not seen Lady Macbeth since the middle of Act III. At that point (Scene iv) she was still trying to comfort and strengthen her husband (*You lack the season of all natures, sleep* were her last words then), but he was beginning to live a desperate inner life, out of touch with her. Now, after the interval, it is she who cannot sleep and who lives in a fearful world of fantasies.

The scene is introduced in almost documentary prose by the Doctor and the Gentlewoman, preparing the way for Lady Macbeth's contrastingly wild but significant remarks.

1. *watch'd:* stayed up at night to watch.

3. *went into the field:* led his army against the rebels.

4. *throw her nightgown upon her:* The Elizabethans slept naked. A nightgown was what we call a dressing-gown.

5. *closet:* a writing-cabinet. What do you imagine Lady Macbeth wrote?

8–9. *A great perturbation . . . watching!* A terrible disorder, to be asleep yet at the same time to act as though awake!

11. *actual performances:* actions.

14. *meet:* correct, fitting.

15–16. The Gentlewoman has more sense, in Macbeth's Scotland, with secret agents everywhere, than to say anything which can't be conclusively proved.

17. *This is her very guise:* This is exactly as she looked before.

18. *stand close:* stay hidden.

ACT FIVE

SCENE I—*Dunsinane. Macbeth's castle*

Enter a DOCTOR OF PHYSIC *and a* WAITING-GENTLE-
WOMAN

Doctor

I have two nights watch'd with you, but can perceive
no truth in your report. When was it she last walk'd?

Gentlewoman

Since his Majesty went into the field, I have seen her
rise from her bed, throw her nightgown upon her,
unlock her closet, take forth paper, fold it, write 5
upon't, read it, afterwards seal it, and again return to
bed; yet all this while in a most fast sleep.

Doctor

A great perturbation in nature, to receive at once the
benefit of sleep and do the effects of watching! In this
slumb'ry agitation, besides her walking and other 10
actual performances, what, at any time, have you
heard her say?

Gentlewoman

That, sir, which I will not report after her.

Doctor

You may to me; and 'tis most meet you should.

Gentlewoman

Neither to you nor any one, having no witness to con- 15
firm my speech.

Enter LADY MACBETH, *with a taper*

Lo you, here she comes! This is her very guise; and,
upon my life, fast asleep. Observe her; stand close.

20-1. There is a horrible irony in the fact that the woman who said *Come, thick night, And pall thee in the dunnest smoke of hell* (Act I, Scene v, lines 50–1) should now be, like a nervous child, afraid of the dark. On the other hand it might be said that she herself is now *in the dunnest smoke of hell*.

24-8. She stops at this point, puts down the candle, and stands desperately going through the motions of washing—an *accustomed action* since her 'nervous breakdown'.

29. *Yet:* still, even now.
a spot: of blood (though she had told her husband *A little water clears us of this deed,* Act II, Scene ii, line 67).

31. *satisfy my remembrance:* back up and confirm what I remember later.

32. *One, two:* either the bell she struck as a signal for Macbeth (Act II, Scene i, lines 31–2) or, more likely, the clock striking in the night when Duncan was murdered.

33. *Hell is murky:* i.e. the hell she is now in. Her broken speeches are a mixture of unnaturally 'tough' comments like those she made when she was inciting her husband to crime, and fearful remarks which represent the sensitive womanly nature she deliberately repressed. Do you think we are getting a more accurate picture of her as a person now than when we watched her behaving like a monster before?

39. *The Thane of Fife . . . now?* What effect does the 'nursery rhyme' have on you?

41-2. *you mar all with this starting:* She recalls her anger and dismay when Macbeth broke down at the banquet, and said he saw Banquo's ghost.

43. *Go to, go to:* The Doctor can't resist expressing his deep disapproval of the deeds her words hint at.

Doctor

How came she by that light?

Gentlewoman

Why, it stood by her. She has light by her continually; 20
'tis her command.

Doctor

You see her eyes are open.

Gentlewoman

Ay, but their sense is shut.

Doctor

What is it she does now? Look how she rubs her
hands. 25

Gentlewoman

It is an accustomed action with her, to seem thus
washing her hands; I have known her continue in this
a quarter of an hour.

Lady Macbeth

Yet here's a spot.

Doctor

Hark, she speaks. I will set down what comes from 30
her, to satisfy my remembrance the more strongly.

Lady Macbeth

Out, damned spot! Out, I say! One, two; why then
'tis time to do't. Hell is murky. Fie, my lord, fie! a
soldier, and afeard? What need we fear who knows it,
when none can call our pow'r to account? Yet who 35
would have thought the old man to have had so much
blood in him?

Doctor

Do you mark that?

Lady Macbeth

The Thane of Fife had a wife; where is she now?
What, will these hands ne'er be clean? No more o' 40
that, my lord, no more o' that; you mar all with this
starting.

Doctor

Go to, go to; you have known what you should not.

46–7. *All the perfumes . . . hand:* a close parallel with the similar hopelessness of Macbeth's *Will all great Neptune's ocean wash this blood Clean from my hand?* (Act II, Scene ii, lines 60–1.)

50. *dignity:* value, rank or position.

51–2. Even in such a small part as the Gentlewoman's, Shakespeare gives scope to his players; she has a talent for shrewd and sharp comment.
53. *my practice:* my medical expertise.

58. *out on's grave:* out of his grave.

61–2. *What's done cannot be undone:* There is, again, deep irony in such shoulder-shrugging words coming from a woman broken by the deeds she dismisses.

65. *Foul whisp'rings are abroad:* evil rumours are going around.
65–6. *Unnatural deeds . . . troubles:* the unnatural deeds of leaders like Macbeth lead to unnatural events like rebellion (anything which breaks public order being, in a sense, unnatural).
66. *infected minds:* diseased or corrupted minds, like Lady Macbeth's.

Gentlewoman

She has spoke what she should not, I am sure of that.
Heaven knows what she has known.   45

Lady Macbeth

Here's the smell of the blood still. All the perfumes of
Arabia will not sweeten this little hand. Oh, oh, oh!

Doctor

What a sigh is there! The heart is sorely charg'd.

Gentlewoman

I would not have such a heart in my bosom for the
dignity of the whole body.   50

Doctor

Well, well, well.

Gentlewoman

Pray God it be, sir.

Doctor

This disease is beyond my practice. Yet I have known
those which have walk'd in their sleep who have died
holily in their beds.   55

Lady Macbeth

Wash your hands, put on your nightgown, look not
so pale. I tell you yet again, Banquo's buried; he cannot come out on's grave.

Doctor

Even so?

Lady Macbeth

To bed, to bed; there's knocking at the gate. Come,   60
come, come, come, give me your hand. What's done
cannot be undone. To bed, to bed, to bed.

                              Exit

Doctor

Will she go now to bed?

Gentlewoman

Directly.

Doctor

Foul whisp'rings are abroad. Unnatural deeds   65
Do breed unnatural troubles; infected minds

177

68. She needs a priest to save her soul, rather than a doctor to heal her body.

70. *means of all annoyance:* all means of injuring herself (in particular, of committing suicide).
71. *still:* always, constantly.
72. *mated:* bewildered.

The purpose of this short scene is to show that there are other Scotsmen who are prepared to strive manfully to rid their country of tyranny. Malcolm and Macduff can expect considerable assistance from inside their country, as well as from outside.

3–5. *for their dear causes . . . man:* for the causes they have at heart would rouse even a dead man at a call to fight the bloody battle.

6. *Shall we well meet them:* we are likely to meet them.

8. *file:* list.

10. *unrough:* smooth-cheeked (too young to shave yet).

11. *Protest . . . manhood:* insist on showing (by fighting) that they are now men.

15–16. *He cannot buckle . . . rule:* 'He can no longer impose his will on a failing situation' (the image is of a paunchy man – perhaps swollen with dropsy—trying to control his waistline.)

To their deaf pillows will discharge their secrets.
More needs she the divine than the physician.
God, God forgive us all. Look after her;
Remove from her the means of all annoyance,   70
And still keep eyes upon her. So, good night.
My mind she has mated, and amaz'd my sight.
I think, but dare not speak.

Gentlewoman   Good night, good doctor.

                    Exeunt

SCENE II—*The country near Dunsinane*

          Drum and colours. Enter MENTEITH, CAITHNESS,
                ANGUS, LENNOX *and* SOLDIERS

Menteith
The English pow'r is near, led on by Malcolm,
His uncle Siward, and the good Macduff.
Revenges burn in them; for their dear causes
Would to the bleeding and the grim alarm
Excite the mortified man.

Angus   Near Birnam wood   5
Shall we well meet them; that way are they coming.

Caithness
Who knows if Donalbain be with his brother?

Lennox
For certain, sir, he is not; I have a file
Of all the gentry. There is Siward's son,
And many unrough youths that even now   10
Protest their first of manhood.

Menteith   What does the tyrant?

Caithness
Great Dunsinane he strongly fortifies.
Some say he's mad; others, that lesser hate him,
Do call it valiant fury; but for certain
He cannot buckle his distemper'd cause   15

17. *sticking on his hands:* i.e. the blood shed in the murders.

18–20. *Now minutely . . . love:* Minute by minute men desert him, reflecting and condemning his own treachery (when he betrayed his king). Those who remain technically faithful obey him only because they are under orders, not because they love him.

20–2. *Now does . . . thief:* The play contains some striking images of loose-fitting clothes, of which this is one. They reflect Macbeth's essential inadequacy for the high position he has ruthlessly seized. He has put on royal robes, but he lacks the royal nature to fill them.

22–5. *Who then . . . being there?* Who could blame Macbeth's troubled senses for reacting violently when all his faculties rebel against their owner (i.e. they condemn themselves for belonging to him).

27. *med'cine:* probably, as in French, 'doctor' – referring to Malcolm, who has come to heal the state (*sickly weal*).

28–9. They will shed their blood, which is Scottish, in order to cure Scotland of its disease. (Bleeding was an important form of treatment for many illnesses.)

30. To make Malcolm's cause flourish and to destroy Macbeth and those who support him.

SCENE III

Macbeth is still driving himself on by referring to the most recent prophecies of the witches, but he is increasingly desperate and has little else to encourage him: his wife is mentally ill, he has no real friends, and his castle is being hemmed in by the English forces under Malcolm, Siward and Macduff, and by those Scots who have already rebelled.

1. *let them fly all:* (I don't care) if all my thanes leave me.

3. *taint with fear:* be weakened by the disease of fear.

4–5. *The spirits . . . consequences:* The witches who know everything that is going to happen to human beings.

8. *epicures:* 'luxury-loving people' (derived from debased notions of classical Epicurean philosophy). The tough, hardy Scots perhaps tended to look on the English as pampered Southerners.

9. *sway by:* rule myself with.

Within the belt of rule.
Angus   Now does he feel
His secret murders sticking on his hands;
Now minutely revolts upbraid his faith-breach;
Those he commands move only in command,
Nothing in love. Now does he feel his title   *20*
Hang loose about him, like a giant's robe
Upon a dwarfish thief.
Menteith   Who then shall blame
His pester'd senses to recoil and start,
When all that is within him does condemn
Itself for being there?
Caithness   Well, march we on   *25*
To give obedience where 'tis truly ow'd.
Meet we the med'cine of the sickly weal;
And with him pour we in our country's purge
Each drop of us.
Lennox   Or so much as it needs
To dew the sovereign flower and drown the weeds.   *30*
Make we our march towards Birnam.

Exeunt, marching

SCENE III—*Dunsinane.   Macbeth's castle*

Enter MACBETH, DOCTOR *and* ATTENDANTS

Macbeth
Bring me no more reports; let them fly all.
Till Birnam wood remove to Dunsinane
I cannot taint with fear. What's the boy Malcolm?
Was he not born of woman? The spirits that know
All mortal consequences have pronounc'd me thus: *5*
'Fear not, Macbeth; no man that's born of woman
Shall e'er have power upon thee'. Then fly, false thanes,
And mingle with the English epicures.
The mind I sway by and the heart I bear

11–19. The number of times Macbeth refers to the messenger's (not surprising) paleness is quite astonishing. *cream-fac'd, goose look, prick thy face, and over-red thy fear, lily-liver'd,* possibly *patch* (which can mean 'plaster' as well as 'fool' or 'clown'), *linen cheeks,* and *whey-face.* Such crazy repetitiveness may suggest Macbeth's obsessive nature.
11. *loon:* rogue.

17. *Are counsellors to fear:* make other people afraid.
whey-face: a fellow with a face the colour of skimmed milk.

20. *push:* attack.
21. *cheer:* there is probably a pun here on 'chair', since the two words were pronounced similarly in Elizabethan English. The double meaning would be 'make me cheerful for ever' and 'put me in my chair (throne) for ever'.
disseat: remove from the throne.
22–8. It is some time since the audience has been able to feel any sympathy with Macbeth, but there is real pathos in these lines, emphasized by a quality we have noticed before – a remarkable clear-sightedness when examining himself.
23. *Is fall'n . . . leaf:* Has come to autumn, the time of withered, yellow leaves.
23–6. Macbeth cannot hope to have any of the compensations of old age enjoyed by most reasonably happy men.
27. *mouth-honour:* i.e. respectful words spoken but not meant.
breath: This conveys the same idea.
28. *Which the poor . . . dare not:* Which the faint-hearted speaker would like to hold back.

Shall never sag with doubt nor shake with fear.   10

Enter SERVANT

The devil damn thee black, thou cream-fac'd loon!
Where got'st thou that goose look?
Servant
There is ten thousand—
Macbeth   Geese, villain?
Servant   Soldiers, sir.
Macbeth
Go, prick thy face, and over-red thy fear,
Thou lily-liver'd boy. What soldiers, patch?   15
Death of thy soul! Those linen cheeks of thine
Are counsellors to fear. What soldiers, whey-face?
Servant
The English force, so please you.
Macbeth
Take thy face hence.

Exit SERVANT

                         Seyton!—I am sick at heart,
When I behold—Seyton, I say!—This push   20
Will cheer me ever, or disseat me now.
I have liv'd long enough. My way of life
Is fall'n into the sear, the yellow leaf;
And that which should accompany old age,
As honour, love, obedience, troops of friends,   25
I must not look to have; but, in their stead,
Curses not loud but deep, mouth-honour, breath,
Which the poor heart would fain deny, and dare not.
Seyton!

Enter SEYTON

Seyton
What's your gracious pleasure?
Macbeth   What news more?   30

183

31. Presumably the arrival of the English army, and its size.

35. *moe:* more.
skirr: scour.

37. There is no real need for the doctor to come on until now, and in some productions this is how it is arranged.

40–5. What Macbeth suggests that his wife needs is in the province of a modern psychiatrist, but hardly in that of a medieval doctor.

42. *Raze out:* erase.

43. *oblivious antidote:* a medicine that will make the patient forget.

44. *stuff'd:* overloaded.

47. *physic:* the art of the doctor.
48. Macbeth asked Seyton to help him on with his armour in line 33 (though, according to Seyton, unnecessarily); now he repeats the order irritably. His mind ranges wildly from one thing to another.
staff: the symbol of his rank as commander-in-chief (the equivalent of a modern Field-Marshal's baton).
49. *Doctor . . . from me:* What has this to do with the doctor?
50. *Come, sir, dispatch:* 'Hurry up and get on with it' (addressed to Seyton).
50–1. *cast . . . disease:* diagnose the disease by examining the patient's urine. But the patient now is Scotland; Lady Macbeth has passed from his mind.
52. *pristine health:* the health the country once enjoyed.
pristine: former.
53–4. *I would applaud . . . again:* I would applaud you so enthusiastically that the echoes would then applaud you too.
54. *Pull't off, I say:* Macbeth seems to have changed his mind, and now tells Seyton to take his armour off again.
55. *rhubarb, senna, purgative drugs . . .·* These are all laxatives. Macbeth wants something to purge the body of Scotland of the English intruders, whom he thinks of as poison causing the country's illness. Other Scotsmen, of course, see the English forces as Scotland's medicine.
58. *it:* his armour, or a piece of it.

Seyton
  All is confirm'd, my lord, which was reported.
Macbeth
  I'll fight till from my bones my flesh be hack'd.
  Give me my armour.
Seyton   'Tis not needed yet.
Macbeth
  I'll put it on.
  Send out moe horses, skirr the country round;   35
  Hang those that talk of fear. Give me mine armour.
  How does your patient, doctor?
Doctor   Not so sick, my lord,
  As she is troubled with thick-coming fancies
  That keep her from her rest.
Macbeth   Cure her of that.
  Canst thou not minister to a mind diseas'd,   40
  Pluck from the memory a rooted sorrow,
  Raze out the written troubles of the brain,
  And with some sweet oblivious antidote
  Cleanse the stuff'd bosom of that perilous stuff
  Which weighs upon the heart?
Doctor   Therein the patient   45
  Must minister to himself.
Macbeth
  Throw physic to the dogs—I'll none of it.
  Come, put mine armour on; give me my staff.
  Seyton, send out. Doctor, the thanes fly from me.
  Come, sir, dispatch. If thou couldst, doctor, cast   50
  The water of my land, find her disease,
  And purge it to a sound and pristine health,
  I would applaud thee to the very echo,
  That should applaud again.—Pull't off, I say.—
  What rhubarb, senna, or what purgative drug,   55
  Would scour these English hence? Hear'st thou of them?
Doctor
  Ay, my good lord. Your royal preparation
  Makes us hear something.

59. *bane:* destruction.

61. Probably both 'safe' ('in the clear') and 'unstained by evil'.

The combined Scottish and English forces are now marching towards Dunsinane and are near Birnam Wood.

Stage Direction *colours:* flags.

2. *That chambers will be safe:* i.e. when people can sleep safely in their bedrooms again (unlike Duncan).
doubt it nothing: have no doubt that it will be so.

5. *shadow:* conceal.

6. *host:* army.

6–7. *make discovery . . . of us:* cause the enemy's reconnaissance to make false reports about us.

8–10. *We learn . . . before't:* All reports agree that the confident Macbeth stays all the time in the castle of Dunsinane and will allow us to besiege it (without coming forth to oppose us).

10. *'Tis his main hope:* i.e. to 'sit tight', defending his castle.

11–12. For whenever any opportunity has presented itself, both high and low-ranking soldiers have deserted him . . .

Macbeth   Bring it after me.
  I will not be afraid of death and bane
  Till Birnam Forest come to Dunsinane.   60

                    Exeunt all but the DOCTOR

Doctor
  Were I from Dunsinane away and clear,
  Profit again should hardly draw me here.

                              Exit

SCENE IV—*Before Birnam Wood*

        Drum and colours. Enter MALCOLM, SIWARD, MAC-
        DUFF, SIWARD'S SON, MENTEITH, CAITHNESS, ANGUS,
             LENNOX, ROSS *and* SOLDIERS, *marching*

Malcolm
  Cousins, I hope the days are near at hand
  That chambers will be safe.
Menteith   We doubt it nothing.
Siward
  What wood is this before us?
Menteith   The wood of Birnam.
Malcolm
  Let every soldier hew him down a bough
  And bear't before him; thereby shall we shadow   5
  The numbers of our host, and make discovery
  Err in report of us.
Soldiers   It shall be done.
Siward
  We learn no other but the confident tyrant
  Keeps still in Dunsinane, and will endure
  Our setting down before't.
Malcolm   'Tis his main hope;   10
  For where there is advantage to be given,
  Both more and less have given him the revolt;

13. *constrained things:* wretched creatures forced to obey him.

14–16. *Let our just censures . . . soldiership:* Let us postpone expressing opinions until we see how things turn out. In the meantime let's do our jobs as efficient soldiers.

16–18. *The time approaches . . . we owe:* Soon, when fate has decided the event, we shall be able to distinguish between our expectations (*What we shall say we have*) and our actual achievements (*what we owe*).

19–20. Talking can only raise fragile hopes. Fighting (*strokes*) is the way to decide the issue beyond doubt.

SCENE V

Macbeth does at first seem the *confident tyrant* that Siward called him. It appears that he has come through his old misgivings and fears to a state of tough indifference. Is this impression confirmed as the scene goes on, or are there deeper, different emotions in the man?

3. *let them lie:* let the besieging forces stay.

4. *ague:* fever (infectious fevers of several kinds were very common in armies in those days).

5. *forc'd:* reinforced.

those that should be ours: Macbeth's way of referring to the *more and less* who *have given him the revolt.*

6. *dareful:* defiantly.

beard to beard: face to face.

10–13. *The time has been . . . were in't:* 'Formerly I would have shivered with fear at a cry in the night, and the hair would have stood up on my scalp as though it had a life of its own, when I heard a horrifying story.'

fell: formerly used of any skin with fur or hair on it.

And none serve with him but constrained things
Whose hearts are absent too.

Macduff   Let our just censures
Attend the true event, and put we on   *15*
Industrious soldiership.

Siward   The time approaches
That will with due decision make us know
What we shall say we have, and what we owe.
Thoughts speculative their unsure hopes relate,
But certain issue strokes must arbitrate;   *20*
Towards which advance the war.

Exeunt, marching

SCENE V—*Dunsinane.   Macbeth's castle*

Enter MACBETH, SEYTON *and* SOLDIERS, *with drum and colours*

Macbeth

Hang out our banners on the outward walls;
The cry is still 'They come'. Our castle's strength
Will laugh a siege to scorn. Here let them lie
Till famine and the ague eat them up.
Were they not forc'd with those that should be ours,   *5*
We might have met them dareful, beard to beard,
And beat them backward home.

A cry within of women

                                   What is that noise?

Seyton

It is the cry of women, my good lord. [*Exit*]

Macbeth

I have almost forgot the taste of fears.
The time has been my senses would have cool'd   *10*
To hear a night-shriek, and my fell of hair
Would at a dismal treatise rouse and stir

14-15. *Direness . . . start me:* Horror, which has become commonplace in my murderous thoughts, has no power ever to startle me now.

17-28. Although he seemed concerned about his wife's health in Scene iii, his reaction to the news of her death is one of indifference. It prompts him to a kind of hymn to futility – marvellous poetry expressing complete negation. (Perhaps the *cry of women* suggests that Lady Macbeth committed suicide. This is largely confirmed by Malcolm in the last speech of the play.)

17-18. It would have been better if she had died later on, at a more convenient time for such news.

19. Shakespeare's flexible use of his normal verse-line (a decasyllable, or five-footed line) is demonstrated throughout his plays, but this one is almost shockingly effective. Notice how well it conveys the plodding monotony of dreary days succeeding each other in a meaningless life.

21. *To the last syllable . . . time:* i.e. until the very last word of human history is written.

22-3. *And all . . . death:* And every day in the past stupid human beings have been able to see just well enough to move to their deaths and crumble to dust in their graves.

23. *Out, out, brief candle!* Macbeth's farewell to his wife. In the *Book of Job* (18, vi) the word *candle* is used to symbolize the light of life in a wicked person.

24-6. *walking shadow* and *poor player:* both are ways of referring to an actor. Shakespeare often refers to his own profession in a way which stresses the unreality of acting and the impossibility of presenting life meaningfully on the stage. Certainly the emphasis here is upon the pointlessness of human life.

25. *struts and frets:* the activity is hectic, but in no way significant.

26-8. *it is a tale . . . nothing:* a statement of extreme cynicism and despair. The whole point of the last part of the play is to contrast Macbeth's negativeness and wickedness with the hope of new life, energy, orderliness and goodness under Malcolm.

29. Do you think there should be a long pause after Macbeth's last words?

30. *Gracious my lord:* 'My gracious lord.' Although there is no sign of grace in Macbeth now he is still the king and must be addressed in an appropriate manner.

As life were in't. I have supp'd full with horrors;
Direness, familiar to my slaughterous thoughts,
Cannot once start me.

Re-enter SEYTON

                         Wherefore was that cry?   15
Seyton
The Queen, my lord, is dead.
Macbeth
                She should have died hereafter;
There would have been a time for such a word.
To-morrow, and to-morrow, and to-morrow,
Creeps in this petty pace from day to day   20
To the last syllable of recorded time,
And all our yesterdays have lighted fools
The way to dusty death. Out, out, brief candle!
Life's but a walking shadow, a poor player,
That struts and frets his hour upon the stage,   25
And then is heard no more; it is a tale
Told by an idiot, full of sound and fury,
Signifying nothing.

Enter a MESSENGER

Thou com'st to use thy tongue; thy
story quickly.
Messenger
Gracious my lord,   30
I should report that which I say I saw,
But know not how to do't.
Macbeth   Well, say, sir.
Messenger
As I did stand my watch upon the hill,
I look'd toward Birnam, and anon methought
The wood began to move.
Macbeth   Liar and slave!   35
Messenger
Let me endure your wrath, if't be not so.

37. *three mile:* We still sometimes use singular forms in recording measurements, e.g. 'he's six foot two'.

39. *next:* nearest.

40. *Till famine cling thee:* Until starvation shrivels you up.
If thy speech be sooth: If what you say is true.

41. I don't care if you do the same to me (i.e. bind me alive to a tree).

42–4. *I pull in . . . like truth:* I find my determination checked and I begin to wonder whether the Devil (speaking in the form of the Third Apparition, the Child Crowned) was misleading me by lying, though seeming to tell the truth.

46. *Arm, arm, and out:* He shouts orders to make an attack on the besieging army.

47–8. *If this . . . tarry here:* i.e. If what this messenger says is true, it won't make any difference whether we try to escape or stay here in the castle.

49. *gin:* begin.

50. *th'estate o' th' world:* 'the ordered universe'. This is the familiar need of the insane dictator – to pull everything down in ruins when he himself is destroyed.

51. *the alarum bell:* the bell warning the men in the castle that an attack is coming.
wrack: destruction. Compare the common phrase 'wrack and ruin'.

52. *harness:* armour. Macbeth regains a touch of his old courage and zest for battle.

SCENE VI

Malcolm is already showing the calmness and confidence of genuine authority.

1. *leavy:* leafy.

2. *show like those you are:* i.e. the soldiers are to reveal themselves; the camouflage has served its purpose.

4. *battle:* section of the army.
Notice that Malcolm now uses the royal *we*. He is growing into his properly inherited role.

6. *our order:* our plan of battle.

7–8. If we can only bring the tyrant's army to battle tonight we will accept defeat if we cannot fight worthily.

Within this three mile may you see it coming;
I say, a moving grove.
Macbeth   If thou speak'st false,
Upon the next tree shalt thou hang alive,
Till famine cling thee. If thy speech be sooth,   *40*
I care not if thou dost for me as much.
I pull in resolution, and begin
To doubt th' equivocation of the fiend
That lies like truth. 'Fear not, till Birnam wood
Do come to Dunsinane.' And now a wood   *45*
Comes toward Dunsinane. Arm, arm, and out.
If this which he avouches does appear,
There is nor flying hence nor tarrying here.
I gin to be aweary of the sun,
And wish th' estate o' th' world were now undone.   *50*
Ring the alarum bell. Blow wind, come wrack;
At least we'll die with harness on our back.

Exeunt

SCENE VI—*Dunsinane.   Before the castle*

Drum and colours. Enter MALCOLM, SIWARD, MAC-
DUFF *and their* ARMY *with boughs*

Malcolm

Now near enough; your leavy screens throw down,
And show like those you are. You, worthy uncle,
Shall with my cousin, your right noble son,
Lead our first battle; worthy Macduff and we
Shall take upon's what else remains to do,   *5*
According to our order.
Siward   Fare you well.
Do we but find the tyrant's power to-night,
Let us be beaten, if we cannot fight.
Macduff
Make all our trumpets speak; give them all breath,

10. *clamorous harbingers:* noisy heralds, or forerunners.

bear being bended

SCENE VII 7

Battle is about to be joined. Macbeth is still depending on the only saying of the witches that has not yet been proved false (*none of woman born Shall harm Macbeth*, Act IV, Scene i, lines 79–80).

The battle is presented in the usual manner of the Elizabethan and Jacobean stage. Brief incidents, involving very small numbers of combatants, succeed each other rapidly, to produce a sense of excitement and expectation in the audience.

1–2. The image is from a favourite Elizabethan sport, bear-baiting, in which a bear was tied to a stake while dogs attacked it.
course: a round or bout.

6–7. It sounds as though Young Siward already suspects that he is facing Macbeth.

10. *abhorred:* hated, loathed.
10–11. *with my sword . . . thou speak'st:* I'll show you by the way I fight that you lie in suggesting I'm afraid of your name.

12–13. Macbeth still seems invincible. Certainly he has once more convinced himself that he is.

Those clamorous harbingers of blood and death.

Exeunt

SCENE VII—*Another part of the field*

Enter MACBETH

Macbeth
They have tied me to a stake; I cannot fly,
But bear-like I must fight the course. What's he
That was not born of woman? Such a one
Am I to fear, or none.

Enter YOUNG SIWARD

Young Siward
What is thy name?
Macbeth   Thou'lt be afraid to hear it.   5
Young Siward
No; though thou call'st thyself a hotter name
Than any is in hell.
Macbeth   My name's Macbeth.
Young Siward
The devil himself could not pronounce a title
More hateful to mine ear.
Macbeth   No, nor more fearful.
Young Siward
Thou liest, abhorred tyrant; with my sword   10
I'll prove the lie thou speak'st.

Fight, and YOUNG SIWARD *slain*

Macbeth
                        Thou wast born of woman.
But swords I smile at, weapons laugh to scorn,
Brandish'd by man that's of a woman born.

Exit. Alarums. Enter MACDUFF

16. *still:* for ever.

17. *kerns:* Irish foot-soldiers, paid to fight, as Macduff says. (They were previously mentioned as members of Macdonwald's army, Act I, Scene ii, line 13).

18. *staves:* shafts of spears, and therefore the spears themselves.

18–20. *either thou, Macbeth . . . undeeded:* Macduff now will not fight anyone but Macbeth. His overwhelming desire is to take revenge for the fate of his family.

20. *undeeded:* without having done any deeds in battle.

There thou shouldst be: That's where you're likely to be.

22. *bruited:* announced by noise.

Stage Direction *Exit:* Macduff goes off, seeking Macbeth, and the audience is left in suspense as to the consequence.

24. *The castle's gently render'd:* 'The castle has been surrendered with remarkably little resistance'. (No doubt, as soon as Macbeth left it, there was little incentive for the defenders to continue fighting.)

25. We have already heard, from Macbeth himself, that many of his men have gone over to the other side (Act V, Scene iii, lines 7–8). The process must have accelerated by now.

27. *The day . . . yours:* i.e. Your victory is now almost won.

28–9. *foes That strike beside us:* enemy soldiers who deliberately miss us when they strike.

SCENE VIII

Macbeth's death leaves mixed feelings in most people's minds. You will find this discussed in the Summing-up.

1. *play the Roman fool:* When an honourable Roman faced defeat he usually thought it his duty to commit suicide (see Shakespeare's *Julius Caesar*).

2–3. *Whiles I see lives . . . upon them:* As long as I see live enemies, mortal wounds are better in them than in me.

Macduff

    That way the noise is. Tyrant, show thy face.
    If thou beest slain and with no stroke of mine,   *15*
    My wife and children's ghosts will haunt me still.
    I cannot strike at wretched kerns whose arms
    Are hir'd to bear their staves; either thou, Macbeth,
    Or else my sword with an unbattered edge
    I sheathe again undeeded. There thou shouldst be;   *20*
    By this great clatter, one of greatest note
    Seems bruited. Let me find him, Fortune,
    And more I beg not.

      Exit. Alarums. Enter MALCOLM *and* OLD SIWARD

Siward

    This way, my lord. The castle's gently rend'red;
    The tyrant's people on both sides do fight;   *25*
    The noble thanes do bravely in the war;
    The day almost itself professes yours,
    And little is to do.

Malcolm   We have met with foes
    That strike beside us.

Siward   Enter, sir, the castle.

      Exeunt. Alarum

SCENE VIII—*Another part of the field*

      Enter MACBETH

Macbeth

    Why should I play the Roman fool, and die
    On mine own sword? Whiles I see lives, the gashes
    Do better upon them.

      Enter MACDUFF

Macduff   Turn, hell-hound, turn.

4. *Of all men else:* More than any other man.

5–6. *my soul . . . already:* Are we to take this as a sign of lingering human feelings (remorse, for example) in Macbeth? Does the comment change your attitude to him at this point?

8. *terms:* words.
Thou losest labour: You're wasting your efforts.

9–10. You can just as easily make a mark with your sharp sword on the uncuttable air as make me bleed.
10. *vulnerable crests:* the helmets of men who can be wounded.

12. *a charmed life:* a life protected by a magic spell.
must not: cannot.

13. *Despair thy charm:* Give up faith in your magical protection.

14. *angel:* evil spirit. (Angels could be good or bad.)
still: always.

16. *Untimely:* prematurely (i.e. before he was ready to be born naturally).

18. *cow'd my better part of man:* crushed my spirit.

19. *juggling:* cheating.

20. 'That trick us by saying things that have two meanings'. This is the point at which Macbeth finally gives up reliance on the witches. After a moment of foreboding and fear he falls back on his native courage and dies fighting bravely.
21–2. *That keep the word . . . our hope!* i.e. their words turn out to be literally true, but the other possible meaning, which inspired hope, proves false.
24. *the show and gaze o' th' time:* a popular public spectacle (as at a fair).
25. *rarer monsters:* 'strangest freaks'. Monsters, in this sense, such as calves with two heads, were frequently shown at fairs.
26. Sideshows were advertised by paintings on cloth hung from poles. Macduff goes on to describe the caption written under the picture.
27. *Here:* in the tent where the freak is exhibited.

29. *baited with the rabble's curse:* irritated by the crowd's curses (Macbeth is again comparing himself with a bear; see Scene vii, lines 1–2).
31. *And thou oppos'd:* And though you are here opposed to me.

Macbeth
    Of all men else I have avoided thee.
    But get thee back; my soul is too much charg'd   5
    With blood of thine already.
Macduff   I have no words—
    My voice is in my sword: thou bloodier villain
    Than terms can give thee out.

Fight. Alarum

Macbeth   Thou losest labour.
    As easy mayst thou the intrenchant air
    With thy keen sword impress as make me bleed.   10
    Let fall thy blade on vulnerable crests;
    I bear a charmed life, which must not yield
    To one of woman born.
Macduff   Despair thy charm;
    And let the angel whom thou still hast serv'd
    Tell thee Macduff was from his mother's womb   15
    Untimely ripp'd.
Macbeth
    Accursed be that tongue that tells me so,
    For it hath cow'd my better part of man;
    And be these juggling fiends no more believ'd
    That palter with us in a double sense,   20
    That keep the word of promise to our ear,
    And break it to our hope! I'll not fight with thee.
Macduff
    Then yield thee, coward,
    And live to be the show and gaze o' th' time.
    We'll have thee, as our rarer monsters are,   25
    Painted upon a pole, and underwrit
    'Here may you see the tyrant'.
Macbeth   I will not yield,
    To kiss the ground before young Malcolm's feet
    And to be baited with the rabble's curse.
    Though Birnam wood be come to Dunsinane,   30
    And thou oppos'd, being of no woman born,

32. *Yet I will try the last:* I will nevertheless go to the very limit (that is, fight to the death).
32–3. *Before my body . . . shield:* i.e. I hold my shield in front of my body.
33. *Lay on:* fight.

35. Malcolm is referring to men who have not reported from the battle – that is, those who may have been killed or wounded.

36. *go off:* be killed.
by these I see: judging by the (number of) men I see around here . . .

38. *your noble son:* Young Siward.

39. *paid a soldier's debt:* 'given his life'. (A soldier virtually undertakes to do this, if necessary, when he enters his profession.)
40. I.e. he had only just become an adult.
41–3. *The which no sooner . . . died:* Immediately he had proved his manhood by his fighting quality in carrying out his duty without shrinking, there and then he died like a man.

46–50. Siward's reaction to his son's death is a tough soldier's attitude, but undoubtedly sincere. It is typical of men dedicated to service and is not unlike Macbeth's own view of the soldier's profession when he was honoured and praised at the beginning of the play.

48. *hairs:* a pun on 'heirs' – another example of a serious pun, a thing we no longer accept as part of the dramatist's art.

50. *his knell is knoll'd:* his death-bell has been tolled (that is, all necessary formalities have been carried out).

52. *parted:* departed.
paid his score: settled all his debts (by doing his duty as a soldier).

Yet I will try the last. Before my body
I throw my warlike shield. Lay on, Macduff;
And damn'd be him that first cries 'Hold, enough!'

Exeunt, fighting. Alarums
Retreat and flourish. Enter, with drum and colours,
MALCOLM, SIWARD, ROSS, LENNOX, ANGUS, CAITHNESS,
MENTEITH *and* SOLDIERS

Malcolm
I would the friends we miss were safe arriv'd.   35
Siward
Some must go off; and yet, by these I see,
So great a day as this is cheaply bought.
Malcolm
Macduff is missing, and your noble son.
Ross
Your son, my lord, has paid a soldier's debt:
He only liv'd but till he was a man;   40
The which no sooner had his prowess confirm'd
In the unshrinking station where he fought,
But like a man he died.
Siward   Then he is dead?
Ross
Ay, and brought off the field. Your cause of sorrow
Must not be measur'd by his worth, for then   45
It hath no end.
Siward   Had he his hurts before?
Ross
Ay, on the front.
Siward   Why, then, God's soldier be he!
Had I as many sons as I have hairs,
I would not wish them to a fairer death.
And so his knell is knoll'd.
Malcolm   He's worth more sorrow,   50
And that I'll spend for him.
Siward   He's worth no more.
They say he parted well and paid his score;

201

55. *The time:* The world in our time.

56. *compass'd with thy kingdom's pearl:* surrounded by the jewels of your kingdom (the faithful thanes standing around).

57. i.e. they are all thinking what Macduff is putting into words.

61. 'Before I, the king, settle the debt I owe you, by rewarding you for your services'.

The short time he mentions is in fact only a few seconds. He rewards them by making them earls. This action also symbolizes his gratitude to King Edward of England, because the rank of earl was an English one.

64–5. *What's more . . . time:* Whatever else I have to do, which ought to be begun appropriately in a new régime . . .

68. *Producing forth:* Finding and arresting.

69. Is Malcolm's summing-up of Macbeth and his wife an adequate obituary for them? Is this how you feel about them?

70–1. *by self . . . her life:* committed suicide.

72. *by the grace of Grace:* The personification of grace is God himself.

73. *in measure, time and place:* 'in the right proportion, at the right time, in the right place'. Malcolm is the restorer of order in Scottish society.

And so, God be with him! Here comes newer comfort.

Re-enter MACDUFF, *with* MACBETH'S *head*

Macduff

    Hail, King! for so thou art. Behold where stands
    Th' usurper's cursed head. The time is free.   55
    I see thee compass'd with thy kingdom's pearl
    That speak my salutation in their minds;
    Whose voices I desire aloud with mine—
    Hail, King of Scotland!

All

                      Hail, King of Scotland! [*Flourish*]

Malcolm

    We shall not spend a large expense of time   60
    Before we reckon with your several loves,
    And make us even with you. My Thanes and kinsmen,
    Henceforth be Earls, the first that ever Scotland
    In such an honour nam'd. What's more to do,
    Which would be planted newly with the time—   65
    As calling home our exil'd friends abroad
    That fled the snares of watchful tyranny;
    Producing forth the cruel ministers
    Of this dead butcher, and his fiend-like queen,
    Who, as 'tis thought, by self and violent hands   70
    Took off her life—this, and what needful else
    That calls upon us, by the grace of Grace,
    We will perform in measure, time, and place.
    So thanks to all at once and to each one,
    Whom we invite to see us crown'd at Scone.   75

Flourish. Exeunt

SUMMING UP

The man Macbeth He is the first person named in the
play, and with his wife, the last to be referred to: *this dead
butcher, and his fiend-like queen*. The play is, in a very real
sense, about a man named Macbeth. Lady Macbeth is
interesting and influential, but Macbeth is the centre of
attention throughout. If your final judgment of him is
similar to Malcolm's *this dead butcher*, you will probably
have found the play both fascinating and horrifying. But
it is likely that you will have seen more in him than that –
perhaps felt the tragedy of the decline and ruin of a brave,
talented, even affectionate man, and understood something
of the mystery of good and evil mingled in human experience.

It is the witches who mention him first, and that within
ten lines of the beginning. After associating themselves with
disturbance in the elements (*In thunder, lightning, or in
rain?*) and with human confusion (*When the battle's lost
and won*), they significantly state their intention to *meet with
Macbeth*. So, from the start, there is a question mark
against the man: what can such evil creatures want with a
Scottish hero fresh from his greatest triumph? They speak
almost as though they have an appointment with him, or he
with them. In contrast, in the second scene, Macbeth
receives glowing commendation from the Sergeant, from
King Duncan and from Ross, but it is noticeable that the
sole basis of the recommendation is his tremendous fighting
spirit, amounting to unique ferocity. The Sergeant becomes
incoherent in his efforts to describe the behaviour of
Macbeth and Banquo on the battlefield. He is forced into
comparisons which certainly make a doubtful impression
on modern readers:

> *Except they meant to bathe in reeking wounds,*
> *Or memorize another Golgotha,*
> *I cannot tell* –

(Act I, Scene ii, lines 39-41)

Even in an age when military prowess was more whole-
heartedly admired than in our own, surely a conflict so

bloody as to recall the Crucifixion, with all that has meant
to Christians throughout the centuries, must raise questions
about the motives of those involved?

There is the same suggestion of abnormally violent
courage in Ross's address to Macbeth when he brings the
news that the king has made him Thane of Cawdor:

> Nothing afeard of what thyself didst make,
> Strange images of death.

> (Act I Scene iii, lines 97-8)

Banquo is soon cleared of any suspicion by his loyalty to
the good Duncan and by his self-identification with the
divine:

> In the great hand of God I stand, and thence
> Against the undivulg'd pretence I fight
> Of treasonous malice

> (Act II, Scene iii, lines 130-2)

His partner, however, from the time of the first encounter
with the witches (that is, on the very first occasion when we
see him) responds to tests and temptations very differently.
Banquo unhesitatingly associates the witches with the devil:

> What can the devil speak true?

> (Act I, Scene iii, line 108)

Macbeth, however, on hearing the first prophecies, seems
afraid and, when the first one comes true so quickly and
unexpectedly, sinks into a troubled reverie full of night-
marish visions (Act I, Scene iii, lines 131-43). The two men,
heroes of the war, are already differentiated, their paths
already diverging.

Macbeth and destiny   One other aspect of the early
impression made by Macbeth must be mentioned. The
Sergeant commented (Act I, Scene ii, lines 14-24) that
Macbeth disdained Fortune when he pursued and killed the
traitor Macdonwald in the battle. There is a significant
distinction to be made here: to defy Fortune in such a
cause is widely and perhaps rightly admired. But there is a
state of mind in which a man may stubbornly refuse to
accept anything which destiny seems to hold out to him.
In this state of mind a man may strike out wildly in every
direction and on every occasion, until he is finally over-

whelmed by disillusion and despair. This is Macbeth's mentality, as opposed to Banquo's, and it is well illustrated when the first prophecy of the witches comes true. Banquo talks about trust:

> *That, trusted home,*
> *Might yet enkindle you unto the crown . . .*
>
> (Act I, Scene iii, lines 121-2)

while Macbeth immediately considers assisting Fortune by committing murder:

> *My thought, whose murder yet is but fantastical,*
> *Shakes so my single state of man*
> *That function is smother'd in surmise,*
> *And nothing is but what is not.*
>
> (Act I, Scene iii, lines 140-3)

He brushes aside the 'accepting' thought that his destiny may in any case be a great one:

> *If chance will have me King, why, chance may crown me,*
> *Without my stir.*
>
> (Act I, Scene iii, lines 145-6)

and takes things into his own hands.

Macbeth's view of right and wrong. If Macbeth is presented, from the very beginning of the story, as vulnerable to evil promptings from without and from within, it is also clear that he knows right from wrong. Even if the balance of his mind is at times disturbed, he is not the sort of criminal who could or would plead that he didn't know what he was doing. In the soliloquy *If it were done when 'tis done . . .* (Act I, Scene vii, lines 1-28) he takes it for granted that a king should be able to trust one of his subjects, and particularly a man who is also his relative and his host, to protect and cherish him – certainly not to murder him in his sleep. Further, Macbeth has a positive appreciation of Duncan's human qualities:

> *this Duncan*
> *Hath borne his faculties so meek, hath been*
> *So clear in his great office*
>
> (Act I, Scene vii, lines 16-18)

and, at the end of his terrible career, his underlying sense of what is true and fitting reasserts itself when he speaks

sadly and movingly of the fulfilments of the good life that
he has cast away:

> *. . . that which should accompany old age,*
> *As honour, love, obedience, troops of friends,*
> *I must not look to have . . .*

(Act V, Scene iii, lines 24-6)

The meaning of manliness   Another important question
for us, as observers of the play, is this: how can a man
who knows the meaning of love, honour and virtue, who
admires his truly admirable king and fights bravely for him,
destroy that same king in a most treacherous way. How
can he then go on to destroy his best friend, and many
others, including women and children? The answer seems
to lie in deep confusion about what being a man means.
This, of course, links up directly with the image of the
ferocious soldier in the first few scenes, which we examined
in the first section of this summing-up. There have been
men in our own century who were honoured and praised
for violent deeds in war, but who failed to adjust to peace-
time, having acquired a taste for violence, and became
deadly criminals. Macbeth seems to be in this category.
Some might want to delve a little deeper into the character
of such a man and say that he was one who had to prove
something to himself. In this connection it is interesting to
see that, just after he has uttered the true and heartfelt
words:

> *I dare do all that may become a man;*
> *Who dares do more is none.*

(Act I, Scene vii, lines 46-7)

in reply to Lady Macbeth's fierce taunting, he is almost
immediately converted to committing the murder by her
twisted definition of manliness (in the course of which she
horribly denies her own essential womanliness):

> *When you durst do it, then you were a man;*
> *And to be more than what you were, you would*
> *Be so much more the man . . .*
> *   I have given suck, and know*
> *How tender 'tis to love the babe that milks me –*
> *I would, while it was smiling in my face,*
> *Have pluck'd my nipple from his boneless gums,*

> *And dash'd the brains out, had I so sworn*
> *As you have done to this.*
>
> (Act I, Scene vii, lines 49-59)

The same warped reasoning is used when Macbeth bullies
the murderers into killing Banquo. His strange speech
about the various kinds of dogs, lifted from its context,
might be thought to be an exhortation by an honourable
man to other potentially honourable men:

> *. . . If you have a station in the file,*
> *Not i' th' worst rank of manhood, say't;*
>
> (Act III, Scene i, lines 100-1)

and again:

> *Your spirits shine through you.*
>
> (Act III, Scene i, line 126)

The whole elaborate image presents a world in which
bounteous nature has arranged an appropriate function for
every creature, and in which leaders can respect and love
their subjects, grappling them *to the heart and love of us*, as
Macbeth himself puts it. But the man who speaks is a foul
tyrant and he is speaking to hired thugs. The speaker's main
argument is that any man who allows himself to be ruled by
patience when he is – supposedly – being ill-treated by
another, can't call himself a man at all. It is exactly the
same argument that was so effective when used on Macbeth
by his wife.

Macbeth's increasing self-centredness During the course
of the play Macbeth moves from preoccupation with himself and his situation to total self-obsession. At no point
does he seem to be a man who relates easily to others.
Banquo, his fellow-soldier, who has shared the kind of
experiences that bind men together, calls him *Worthy
Macbeth* and *My noble partner*, but they do not seem to be
close friends. The only person to whom Macbeth talks
freely – at first – is his wife, though the way they speak to
each other is curious. Nearly all Lady Macbeth's forms of
address to her husband refer to his rank or title: *Great
Glamis, worthy Cawdor, worthy Thane, my royal Lord;* only
once does she call him husband. He, on the other hand, is
usually much more affectionate; *my dearest partner, my
dearest love, dear wife, dearest chuck*. The contrast suggests

that Lady Macbeth's feeling for her husband has come to be expressed overwhelmingly in terms of attention to his 'getting on in the world' (like a modern wife who – with 'ulterior motives' – invites her husband's boss to dinner), a concentration which leads her to a deliberate appeal to evil spirits to *unsex* her, and symbolically to pervert her own maternal instincts:

> . . . *Come to my woman's breasts,*
> *And take my milk for gall, you murd'ring ministers . . .*
>
> (Act I, Scene v, lines 47-8)

Macbeth, however, seems to look upon his marriage-partner primarily as a wife and the potential mother of his children:

> *Bring forth men-children only . . .*
>
> (Act I, Scene vii, line, 73)

A well-known critic, Mr L. C. Knights, once made fun of other critics of a pedantic kind by pointing out how futile it is to wonder how many children Lady Macbeth had had (since she said she had *given suck*). All that really matters is that there is no sign of a young Macbeth to inherit the throne of Scotland; that Macbeth is very much concerned that the prophecy about Banquo's children should not come true, and that he no doubt hopes for an heir (to fight as he does, Macbeth must be a young man: modern stage make-up often obscures this truth). This makes Lady Macbeth's denial or distortion of her sexuality particularly unfortunate for him. They begin to drift apart before the death of Banquo (see Act III, Scene ii). The partnership in greatness they had both looked forward to comes to nothing. The deed divides them, and Macbeth is left to brood darkly on further crimes, an even more lonely man than before. His wife asks:

> *Why do you keep alone,*
> *Of sorriest fancies your companions making?*
>
> (Act III, Scene ii, lines 8-9)

At this mid-point in the play, then, with Banquo's death already planned, three of Macbeth's most significant characteristics, all related to each other, have become accentuated. He is more withdrawn and out of touch with his fellow human beings; he relies less and less on *Fortune* or destiny to direct the course of his life, and yet, as a paradoxical consequence, has less and less control over it; and he puts even more trust than before in violence as the only solution. In other words, he is becoming perceptibly less human. All this is well illustrated in the banquet scene (Act III, Scene iv); throughout he is trying desperately to act a part – the part of Duncan, the king he has killed and replaced – and failing. Macbeth's words and actions are designed to convey the benevolence of a confident ruler of a society in which the subjects know their *own degrees* and serve in mutual respect and love. But first he has to excuse himself to hear what the murderers have to say about the fate of Banquo and Fleance; then Banquo's ghost comes to haunt him at the moment when Macbeth is trying hardest to seem hospitable and natural:

> *Here had we now our country's honour roof'd,*
> *Were the grac'd person of our Banquo present;*
>> (Act III, Scene iv, lines 40-1)

> *I drink to the general joy o' th' whole table,*
> *And to our dear friend Banquo . . .*
>> (Act III, Scene iv, lines 89-90)

Instead of presiding over an occasion to mark a happy state of order in the kingdom, Macbeth has:

> *broke the good meeting,*
> *With most admir'd disorder.*
>> (Act III, Scene iv, lines 109-10)

and from this time onward reduces the entire country to the same sort of chaos, and worse. Indeed, his self-centredness becomes so intense that his words at the end of the banquet scene:

> *For mine own good*
> *All causes shall give way . . .*
>> (Act III, Scene iv, lines 135-6)

become a motto for the rest of his life, amplified in Act IV, Scene i, when he sees the witches again, in a speech of pure megalomania:

> *Though you untie the winds and let them fight*
> *Against the churches; though the yesty waves*
> *Confound and swallow navigation up;*
> *Though bladed corn be lodg'd and trees blown down;*
> *Though castles topple on their warders' heads;*

Though palaces and pyramids do slope
Their heads to their foundations; though the treasure
Of nature's germens tumble all together,
Even till destruction sicken – answer me
To what I ask you.

(Act IV, Scene i, lines 51-60)

Through Shakespeare's skill with words we here see into the soul of all power-crazy men through the ages, from the wilder Roman Emperors to Hitler and Stalin. For although this summing-up began with the statement that the play is 'about a man named Macbeth', it clearly has a wider significance. In Macbeth and his wife are embodied tendencies that are either familiar to us, or accessible to our imaginations. Malcolm's final judgment on the Macbeths as a *dead butcher* and *his fiend-like queen* is perfectly understandable from his point of view, but those who see and read the play are unlikely to dismiss them so sweepingly. Shakespeare's creatures have enabled us to see more deeply into some of the mysteries and contradictions of life.

The side of goodness Long before the end of the play the human tendencies embodied in Macbeth and his wife have been reduced to almost exclusively evil ones. The characters who represent goodness are not nearly so fully individualized. The best two are a king (Duncan) who appears in only three scenes and is dead by the middle of the Second Act, and another king (Edward the Confessor) who never makes an appearance. The two main instruments of Macbeth's downfall, Malcolm and Macduff, are both firmly on the side of goodness by the end, but earlier on they are involved in the confusion of values by their escapes from Scotland, actions which are justified by events but which appear dubious at the time. Banquo, as has already been suggested, seems reluctant to involve himself in action against Macbeth, in spite of his highmindedness. The powers of goodness are conveyed more by symbols and by imagery than by the deeds of individuals comparable in importance to the Macbeths. Nature often illustrates the human and supernatural war that is being waged throughout the play: a study of the varied uses of the word 'nature' can be very illuminating, and some suggestions for such studies are provided in the Theme Index.

The wider context   In spite of the gloom and doubt that pervades most of the scenes, and in spite of the depths of human depravity that are explored, *Macbeth* is a play of hope and faith. There is a fine irony about the ending. The theme of 'appearance and reality', which runs through the story, is almost always used as an instrument of disillusionment. The reality is usually worse than the appearance (Duncan is actually dead, not asleep; Macbeth looks like a real king but isn't) yet the overall impression, that evil has the most powerful weapons and protagonists, proves to be untrue. At the close, Macduff addressing Malcolm, says:

> *The time is free.*
> *I see thee compass'd with thy kingdom's pearl*
>> (Act V, Scene viii, lines 55-6)

and Malcolm himself promises:

> *. . . what needful else*
> *That calls upon us, by the grace of Grace,*
> *We will perform in measure, time, and place.*
>> (Act V, Scene viii, lines 71-3)

There is very much more that could be said about the play; whole books are frequently written on it. The purpose of this summing-up is simply to suggest some of the aspects which are likely to arouse the interest of any thoughtful person. The remaining sections, the Theme Index and the Further Reading list, hint at ways of widening and deepening the reader's approach.

THEME INDEX

Certain themes or recurrent ideas are very noticeable in *Macbeth*, and awareness of them can deepen a reader's understanding of the play. The fundamental notion seems to be the contrast between good and evil, but closely bound up with this is the fact that one can be confused with the other. In other words 'good' and 'evil' sometimes seem ambiguous terms, and this ambiguity may even extend throughout a human being's experience of life. Similarly, there are times when the meanings of words like 'nature' and 'honour' may become blurred, and what one man thinks of as 'order' can be labelled 'repression' by another. During the course of this play such ideas are constantly being presented and represented until, at the end, a glimpse is given of a new and happy 'order' under a trustworthy new king: man's true nature is affirmed, the two meanings of honour come together, and goodness has defeated evil.

The following list of references gives a few examples of the complex way in which Shakespeare presents the contrast and the ambiguity. Some of these examples are overt, that is, they are demonstrated openly or stated directly; others are embedded in the language of the play in the form of images and suggestions. The main division between 'contrast' and 'ambiguity' is only made for convenience; the two ideas frequently overlap.

Contrast

Grace and sin I vi 30; II ii 24-33; II iii 130-2; II iv 40-1; III i 65-8; III i 86-9; III iv 41 & 45; III vi 26-9; IV i 45; IV i 104; IV i 132-3 & 137-8; IV ii 80-1; IV iii 23-4; IV iii 43; IV iii 91-5; IV iii 108-11; IV iii 144-5 & 155-9; IV iii 189-92; V iii 26-7; V viii 71-3.

Hell and heaven I vii 7; II i 63-4; II iii 1-20; III i 139-40; III vi 19; IV iii 223-7; V i 33.

Angels and devils II iii 4 & 7; III iv 59; III vi 45-9; IV iii 22; IV iii 117; V vii 8; V viii 3.

Life and death II ii 6-8; II iii 67-8 & 75-6; II iii 92-7; III ii 19-26; III v 4-5; IV iii 165-6 & 171-3; V viii 39-50.

FURTHER READING

Fuller and more advanced editions of the play are those by Kenneth Muir (New Arden Shakespeare: Methuen/Harvard) and J. Dover Wilson (New Cambridge: C.U.P.). The former contains extracts from Holinshed's chronicle. A. C. Bradley's character-analysis of the play in his *Shakespearean Tragedy* (Macmillan) is still invaluable, and L. C. Knights's famous 'How Many Children had Lady Macbeth?' (in *Explorations*: Penguin) should be read immediately after it.

Cleanth Brooks has an important essay on *Macbeth* in *The Well-Wrought Urn* (Dobson) and E. M. W. Tillyard a sound chapter on it in *Shakespeare's History Plays* (Penguin). Finally, Derek Traversi's chapter on the play in *An Approach to Shakespeare* (Hollis and Carter), Volume II, shows the value of looking at the play as a dramatic poem.

SHAKESPEARE'S LIFE AND TIMES

Very little indeed is known about Shakespeare's private life: the facts included here are almost the only indisputable ones. The dates of Shakespeare's plays are those on which they were first produced.

* * *

1558 Queen Elizabeth crowned.
1561 Francis Bacon born.
1564 Christopher Marlowe born.

1566
1567 Mary, Queen of Scots, deposed.
James VI (later James I of England) crowned King of Scotland.
1572 Ben Jonson born.
Lord Leicester's Company (of players) licensed; later called Lord Strange's, then the Lord Chamberlain's, and finally (under James) The King's Men.
1573 John Donne born.
1574 The Common Council of London directs that all plays and playhouses in London must be licensed.
1576 James Burbage builds the first public playhouse, The Theatre, at Shoreditch, outside the walls of the City.
1577 Francis Drake begins his voyage round the world (completed 1580).
Holinshed's *Chronicles of England, Scotland and Ireland* published (which Shakespeare later used extensively).
1582

William Shakespeare born, April 23rd, baptized April 26th.
Shakespeare's brother, Gilbert, born.

Shakespeare married to Anne Hathaway.

1583 The Queen's Company founded by royal warrant.

Shakespeare's daughter, Susanna, born.

1585

Shakespeare's twins, Hamnet and Judith, born.

1586 Sir Philip Sidney, the Elizabethan ideal 'Christian knight', poet, patron, soldier, killed at Zutphen in the Low Countries.

1587 Mary, Queen of Scots, beheaded.
Marlowe's *Tamburlaine* (*Part I*) first staged.

1588 Defeat of the Spanish Armada.
Marlowe's *Tamburlaine* (*Part II*) first staged.

1589 Marlowe's *Jew of Malta* and Kyd's *Spanish Tragedy* (a 'revenge tragedy' and one of the most popular plays of Elizabethan times).

1590 Spenser's *Faerie Queene* (Books I-III) published.

1592 Marlowe's *Doctor Faustus* and *Edward II* first staged. Witchcraft trials in Scotland.
Robert Greene, a rival playwright, refers to Shakespeare as 'an upstart crow' and 'the only Shake-scene in a country'.

Titus Andronicus
Henry VI, Parts I, II and III
Richard III

1593 London theatres closed by the plague.
Christopher Marlowe killed in a Deptford tavern.

Two Gentlemen of Verona
Comedy of Errors
The Taming of the Shrew
Love's Labour's Lost

1594 Shakespeare's company becomes The Lord Chamberlain's Men.

Romeo and Juliet

1595 Raleigh's first expedition to Guiana. Last expedition of Drake and Hawkins (both died).

Richard II
A Midsummer Night's Dream

1596	Spenser's *Faerie Queene* (Books IV-VI) published. James Burbage buys rooms at Blackfriars and begins to convert them into a theatre.	*King John* *The Merchant of Venice* Shakespeare's son Hamnet dies. Shakespeare's father is granted a coat of arms.
1597	James Burbage dies; his son Richard, a famous actor, turns the Blackfriars Theatre into a private playhouse.	*Henry IV (Part I)* Shakespeare buys and redecorates New Place at Stratford.
1598	Death of Philip II of Spain.	*Henry IV (Part II)* *Much Ado About Nothing*
1599	Death of Edmund Spenser. The Globe Theatre completed at Bankside by Richard and Cuthbert Burbage.	*Henry V* *Julius Caesar* *As You Like It*
1600	Fortune Theatre built at Cripplegate. East India Company founded for the extension of English trade and influence in the East. The Children of the Chapel begin to use the hall at Blackfriars.	*Merry Wives of Windsor* *Troilus and Cressida*
1601		*Hamlet* *Twelfth Night*
1602	Sir Thomas Bodley's library opened at Oxford.	
1603	Death of Queen Elizabeth. James I comes to the throne. Shakespeare's company becomes The King's Men. Raleigh tried, condemned and sent to the Tower.	
1604	Treaty of peace with Spain.	*Measure for Measure* *Othello* *All's Well that Ends Well*
1605	The Gunpowder Plot: an attempt by a group of Catholics to blow up the Houses of Parliament.	
1606	Guy Fawkes and other plotters executed.	*Macbeth* *King Lear*

1607 Virginia, in America, colonized.
A great frost in England.

Antony and Cleopatra
Timon of Athens
Coriolanus
Shakespeare's daughter, Susanna, married to Dr. John Hall.

1608 The company of the Children of the Chapel Royal (who had performed at Blackfriars for ten years) is disbanded.
John Milton born.
Notorious pirates executed in London.

Richard Burbage leases the Blackfriars Theatre to six of his fellow actors, including Shakespeare.
Pericles, Prince of Tyre

1609

Shakespeare's *Sonnets* published.

1610 A great drought in England.

Cymbeline

1611 Chapman completes his great translation of the *Iliad*, the story of Troy.
Authorized Version of the Bible published.

A Winter's Tale
The Tempest

1612 Webster's *The White Devil* first staged.

Shakespeare's brother, Gilbert, dies.

1613 Globe Theatre burnt down during a performance of *Henry VIII* (the firing of small cannon set fire to the thatched roof).
Webster's *Duchess of Malfi* first staged.

Henry VIII
Two Noble Kinsmen
Shakespeare buys a house at Blackfriars.

1614 Globe Theatre rebuilt 'in far finer manner than before'.

1616 Ben Jonson publishes his plays in one volume.
Raleigh released from the Tower in order to prepare an expedition to the gold mines of Guiana.

Shakespeare's daughter, Judith, marries Thomas Quiney.
Death of Shakespeare on his birthday, April 23rd.

1618 Raleigh returns to England and is executed on the charge for which he was imprisoned in 1603.

1623 Publication of the Folio edition of Shakespeare's plays.

Death of Anne Shakespeare (née Hathaway).